T0063328

CONVERSATIONS WITH THE WOMB

By Giuditta Tornetta

Best-selling author of Painless Childbirth:
An Empowering Journey Through Pregnancy and Birth

2nd Edition

BALBOA
PRESS
A DIVISION OF HAY HOUSE

Balboa Press books may be ordered through booksellers or by contacting:

Balboa Press
A Division of Hay House
1663 Liberty Drive
Bloomington, IN 47403
www.balboapress.com
1 (877) 407-4847

Because of the dynamic nature of the Internet, any web addresses or
links contained in this book may have changed since publication and
may no longer be valid. The views expressed in this work are solely those
of the author and do not necessarily reflect the views of the publisher,
and the publisher hereby disclaims any responsibility for them.

The author of this book does not dispense medical advice or prescribe the use
of any technique as a form of treatment for physical, emotional, or medical
problems without the advice of a physician, either directly or indirectly. The
intent of the author is only to offer information of a general nature to help
you in your quest for emotional and spiritual well-being. In the event you use
any of the information in this book for yourself, which is your constitutional
right, the author and the publisher assume no responsibility for your actions.

Any people depicted in stock imagery provided by Thinkstock are
models, and such images are being used for illustrative purposes only.
Certain stock imagery © Thinkstock.

Print information available on the last page.

ISBN: 978-1-4525-1563-2 (sc)
ISBN: 978-1-4525-1564-9 (e)

Balboa Press rev. date: 4/24/2015

To my mother Anna, and her womb,
who cuddled me into existence.

Contents

Part I – The Womb

Part II – Nine Chakras of Creation
and the Nine Basic Human Rights

Acknowledgements

First, I'd like to acknowledge the tremendous journey this book has guided me through. I'd like to express my gratitude for the journey, as it miraculously brought me closer to my daughter and has transformed me tremendously since its inception. I often feel the words are not my own, rather channeled in spite of myself. I am indebted to many people who have doulaed and midwifed this book into existence.

The inspiration for *Conversations with the Womb* came from the workshops I have had the privilege to lead all over the world with some amazing teachers.

I want to thank Ibu Robin Lim who has taught me love and service like no one else, and Gloria Gagliardo-De Gast who brightens many of my mornings and helped me realize that, even though I no longer bleed monthly, I needed to pay greater attention to that aspect of my womb. Nicola Goodhall reminded me about sexuality and has been such an amazing resource. We call her Nikipedia for the amazing knowledge she holds. To Ellen Watson who opened my heart to dance and to asking my body to speak to me. My gratitude, love and appreciation to my daughter Natascia Tornetta Mallin. I am so amazed and grateful that God has given me the gift of my daughter, whose no-nonsense commentary and amazing writing skills really transformed this book into a readable work.

I am grateful for my incredibly talented son, Azzurro Tornetta Mallin, who has inspired me to always do better and has worked diligently on each chapter with me and on many of the book exercises. Thank you to my line editors, Monique Ruffin and Jill McKellan. I was so fortunate to meet and collaborate with the talented artist Maritza Torres for the front cover. I fell in love with her art the minute I saw it. I also want to thank all my clients and all the alumni of *Loving the Mother*; without them I could not be who I am today. So many of the words and concepts in this book come from all of you.

I would like to acknowledge the following individuals who I consider my soul sisters and my earth angels: Erin Ryan, Anna Tornetta, Rachel Rosenthal, Barbara Smith, Rachel Love, Elisa Zampetti, Ingrid May, Becky Kopoulsky Gerson, Yana Katzap-Nackman, Diana Payne, Diana Tiffin, Gabriela Angueira, April Fissel, and Christa Cole. A special thanks to the women who work with me, I could not have finished this book had you not been there weekly in my office inspiring me to keep writing and finishing this book. You took such good care of our Joy In Birthing Foundation. I love you Katie Duberg, Caroline McKeown, and Danika Charity.

Giuditta Tornetta
Los Angeles, CA
March 2014

Foreword

Warning: this book is NOT a new-age, self-help softy. Perhaps it's the subject that initially enchanted me. I personally wish *I* had thought of having a Conversation with *my* Womb! Giuditta Tornetta *did* think of it, and she rendered her trailblazing idea into a book that is at once practical, and a wildly esoteric page-turner.

Once I started reading and talking to my own womb, I realized that I had been speaking with *her* all my life. This is the beauty of Giuditta's writing, she's the girlfriend-next-door who comes over with a hot loaf of home baked bread and a bowl of pasta. One whiff and you are brimming over with remembrances of your *own* wisdom. She's *that* good of a neighbor.

Every exercise helped me find authentic questions and answers, concerning my femininity. This book is a journey in the dark, well lit with women's intuition. I found myself laughing out loud, remembering that I personally never had "penis envy." In fact, I felt sorry for people born without a uterus. I mean, why exist with only one brain? What do men think with? Don't get me wrong, I *love* men, am well married to one, and have four sons, who are grown men of wonderful character (and super handsome), but I am *so* happy to have been born a womb-holder.

Her-storically, women were relegated into a squalid societal corner. Men in power bullied us and claimed that we were merely wombs, destined to breed and work our bodies to death as slaves. It was not so simple. The status of individual women was largely dependent upon the economic rank of fathers or husbands. But even royal women were brood mares, only with more sanitized lives, as pretty dolls on shelves, bearing sons. Our Mothers' Mothers struggled for each basic human right – to education, to freedom of expression, to vote, and to have power over our own wombs.

In the tornado vortex of this revolution, women were burned as witches. Perhaps, as a desperate attempt at survival, we put aside our femininity and forgot, or ignored, that we each have a second brain, a thinking, feeling uterus, a rich repository of powerful hormones. Many of us reviled our potential to be healers, mothers, and tender lovers. Some women even resented the womb's miraculous potential to cradle our gestating babies. Irreplaceable as our wombs are, we turned from them demanding all the "rights" that men enjoyed: voting, drinking, smoking, driving, governing, business-ing, etc. Yet, even as a very young person participating in the *Women's Movement*, I noticed that men wore ties to work, and these ties looked to me like nooses.

In the throes of the revolution that gave women some freedom, far too many of us un-friended our uteri. It has been a tragic disconnect. Today, as granddaughters and great granddaughters of the Suffragettes, our legacy includes a plethora of complications, the side-effects of living like men. Our blood pressures are rising and we are having heart attacks because we are not talking to and not listening to our wombs.

What we have rediscovered, with the help of sage women like Giuditta Tornetta, is that our wombs are not our enemy. Small minds creating overpowering policy may harm us, society may attempt to dictate our roles and impede our choices, yet being female, having a uterus, a vagina, breasts, is *not* a curse, it is a blessing beyond compare.

Learning to communicate with my womb brought me remembrances…while gobbling up the knowledge on these pages, I became proud that I made *First Moon Rituals* for my daughters and my granddaughter. I remember them predicting their menarche, excited to discover symptoms that their womanhood was dawning, breast buds, a wisp of new hair in a secret place. This is when I taught my girls to call menstruation their *MoonTime*, their *Resting*. To this day, my grown daughters honor their *Dark Moon Time* by taking a *Red Tent* day off of college or work, and really resting. This downtime gently winds our feminine wellsprings, so that when we emerge after our bleeding, we can leap into our power.

I recalled that my own Filipino mother warned me when I began to bleed: "Our people are not like your father's people. We don't complain when we bleed, we are proud to be female. Our *monthlies*, called *Regla* in our Motherland, are a reminder that we are fertile and powerful. So no complaining! If you make friends with your *Regla*, you will not suffer." I took my Mother's stern wisdom to heart, and I remembered her word. When my first birth contraction arrived, at the beginning of labor with my first baby, I was still a teenager. I do believe her voice in my heart carried me through each contraction, so I did not suffer the pain, but grew and blossomed with each tightening and release.

I like to call our Uteri *Ships of Dreams*, for so much potential is locked safely away in the eggplant-colored place stored deep in our bones. The uterus is the Stargate, through which all saints, beggars, geniuses, truck drivers, ballerinas, and queens must pass through to arrive Earth-side. Now if *that* fact does not knock your socks off, you must be barefoot already!

So many of our sisters have had surgery and lost their Dream Ships. Still more have the deep scar of cesarean birth. A hysterectomy or a cesarean may save your life. Or, it may be an unnecessary operation, done due to a doctor's fear or prejudice or lack of patience. According to Direct Healthcare International: "Hysterectomy is the second most common major surgery among women in the United States. (The most common major surgery that women have is cesarean section delivery.) Each year, more than 600,000 hysterectomies are done. About one third of women in the United States have had a hysterectomy by age 60."

No matter how we lose, or scar a uterus, all women weep with her sisters. And yet, whether your uterus still lives in your pelvis or is gone, Giuditta's book teaches us to talk to her. OK, you may need to speak to your womb long distance, but communicate you must. For we women are hardwired to heal through loving communication.

These pages got me thinking with my uterus, that rebel brain, about DNA: hard copy, chiseled in flesh and bone, the gifts of our earthly ancestors. Epigenesis, on the other hand, is soft copy, the potential to sculpt. Epigenesis is a good reason to protect women in pregnancy, nourish them with plenty of healthy foods, uplifting music, fresh air, fitness movement, and pure happiness. Because human epigenetic expression is sensitive to everything in our environment and everything that enters through the conduit of our senses, the work of Doulas in pregnancy, childbirth and postpartum, cannot be overstated. Loving the Mother protects our future generations. *BirthKeepers* set the stage for each new child to have an intact capacity to love and trust, because dynamic systems are sensitive to start-up conditions.

But Epigenesis does not stop with our primal epiphany. Yes, it is most powerful at the fulcrum of birth, but we keep growing, changing, morphing into ourselves. I believe we can add to who we are, and erase what hurts. This book is a handy tool for self-sculpting, from the deepest inner parts of your female self, *out*. You get to choose, how your epigenetic story will manifest. You can begin to do this, simply by conversing with your Uterus!

Giuditta Tornetta, you are a Butterfly person, who has used the tools you teach so well that your metamorphosis astounds me. Your are: "She Who Holds Sacred Space for Women, in All our Seasons.

~ mOM Shanti, with LOVE, Ibu Robin Lim
Bali, Indonesia - May 2014
2011 CNN Hero of the Year

Preface

Many years ago I found myself at Esalen having a conversation with my shoulder. I was taking a workshop on Rubenfeld's *Synergy Method of Talk and Touch*, which is a modality that integrates bodywork, intuition, and psychotherapy. *Rubenfeld Synergy utilizes talk, movement, awareness, imagination, humor, and compassionate touch as gateways—contacting and melting frozen tensions and emotions, freeing the body from pain and the mind from suffering.* What intrigued me during this experience was the longing I felt coming from my shoulder to communicate with me, and the release and sense of well-being that ensued once that part of my body felt "heard." Scientific research continues to mount showing the truth of a simple principle: the body, mind, emotions, and spirit are dynamically interrelated.

Following that experience, I repeatedly heard different parts of my body calling me to have a conversation with the intention to clear and let go of the emotions and memories that were causing not only emotional but physical pain. Speaking to parts of my body to obtain clarity and healing fascinated me so much that I felt compelled, even called, to speak with my womb.

However, this time, I did not want to simply have a random conversation. My methodical mind longed for an in-depth inquiry where I could touch upon how the many facets of my existence were influencing my womb during the very important life change we call menopause. Taking the time to pause and ask the right questions I chose a tool I call the *Nine Chakras of Creations* that I created when I wrote my first book, *Painless Childbirth*.

The chakras (or energy centers) are used in many healing modalities, especially in Eastern cultures, and have their origins in yoga. What I love about using the chakras is that each relates to a specific physical location in our body as well as a life lesson. In studying the chakras I noticed that many disciplines use them parallel to some basic human rights, like the right to be here, the right to be loved, and the right to speak. I also learned that focusing on each chakra, one at a time, could shed light on obstructions that some life event might have placed on it. Going one by one helped me focus on certain aspects I had not previously considered; and each time I released the energy in a lower chakra I could feel the one above longing for the same relief. This way the conversations with my womb began with questions related to the first chakra: my roots, my relationship with the past, my family of origin, my culture and the tribe I come from. This conversation led me to addressing the second chakra, focusing on feelings my feelings, followed by looking at the relationship with myself in the third chakra: love, intimacy and universal relationships. In the fourth: the impeccability of my words in the fifth; all the way to my relationship with the Divine in the ninth.

The lessons revealed in using the nine basic human rights, in tandem with the lessons embodied in the chakras, helped me follow a specific path. On this path, I was able to see and understand the major influences and belief systems that shaped aspects of my history, my memories, and who I am as a person – a woman, and a mother. By using the nine basic human rights embedded in each chakra, I was able to explore how I truly felt. At times I was surprised that it had taken me all this time to realize that I needed to ask myself if I had a right to have a vision for my life, or if I had a right to my Divine powers. This process helped me shed light into some dark corners I never even knew existed.

Concurrently, for the next five years, I began offering workshops around the world called, *Loving the Mother*, using the *Nine Chakras of Creation* as a tool for healing and self-discovery. During this time, I recognized the value of these tools as I listened to the lively conversations generated from the women who attended my workshops. This is how *Conversations With The Womb* was born.

I am encouraging you to begin an intimate conversation with your own womb, the seat of all creation, and to use the *Nine Chakras of Creation* as a spring board to zero in on what needs your attention.

Through the use of these nine steps you will learn:

- How your history and the pacts you have made in the past affect your present actions.
- How to heal past grief related to your womb and bring to light that which is in the shadows.
- How to use your newfound womb power to take action.
- How to harness the power of intuition, which resides in your womb, and how to listen and trust it.
- How to have a daily conversation with your creative womb.
- How your mind works and what stands in the way of achieving your goals.
- How to harness the power of manifestation.
- How to discover the divine within you.
- How to become one with the creator which is represented in your womb.

Since the journey into our souls requires a lifetime commitment, having frequent reminders has really helped me to stay on track. In this book, when we talk about striving to live a conscious life, or having a conscious contact with the spirit, we tap into a universal message, one that is not *new*, but has been repeated each and every year for centuries by different people using similar kinds of languages. I am not here to impart new knowledge, but to reawaken, remind and/or accompany you on today's journey to self-discovery. Just like athletes practice every day to keep their skill fresh, our spirit needs daily reminders and tools to stay sharp on the journey of self-discovery. Many times, in my fifty-seven years, when I needed inspiration I picked up a book that had motivated me in the past, only to discover that at this particular point in my life I could not read the same message, for my soul was hungry for something new, not a new message per se, but a new shade or voice that would wake up something that was still asleep. In this vein, I offer you these nine steps, the *Nine Chakras of Creation*.

From the title, *Conversations With the Womb*, it would seem that I am only talking to women-folk, but that is not true. I recognize that all human beings have a feminine side to them and that this feminine side needs to be reached through feelings rather than concepts of thought and logical processes, especially when we are going to look at our lives from the holistic point of view encompassing body, mind, spirit, and emotions. So it is to the feminine in all of us that I dedicate this book.

There have been many teachers on my path whose legacies are shared in this book. From Jesus to Siddhartha; Carlos Castaneda to Carolyn Myss; Marianne Williamson to Dr. Christine Northrop; Plato to Bruce Lipton; as well as the women who have given me the privilege to be at the birth of their child; those who have participated in my workshops; the men I have loved; and the one I gave birth to.

My purpose with this book, and in my life's work, is to create an environment where women support one another. I invite you to cultivate nurturing relationships with the supportive people in your life, to join one of our workshops, create a woman's group, or start a book study using this book as your springboard. Then, share how you are doing in these endeavors on my site at <u>www.ConversationsWithTheWomb.com</u>, or on my Facebook page, Conversation With the Womb. Through a loving community, everything is possible.

Introduction

Uterus Mundi

The concept of Uterus Mundi is an adaption of an ancient concept known as Anima Mundi, or World Soul. The world soul is, according to several systems of thought, an intrinsic connection between all living things on the planet. Similar concepts are also held in systems of eastern philosophy in the Brahma-Atman of Hinduism (see story at the end of the book), the Buddha-Nature in Mahayana Buddhism, and in the School of Yin-Yang, Taoism, and Neo-Confucianism as *Chi*. Following the advent of organized religion the search for the anima mundi became a contended realm. In the middle ages, the church and the alchemists explored this concept separately. While the church explained everything as God's creation, the alchemists sought the spirit hidden in matter. Alchemists understood that there was a sacred essence in the fabric of creation, and that it was within and not without. For these beliefs many were persecuted and even killed or burned as heretics. During the renaissance alchemists became scientists and a flourishing of creative energy was responsible for quantum leaps in humankind's history. Later, during the Industrial Revolution, the separation of spirit and matter became once again very strong. This time science ridiculed religion or spirituality, and the once persecuted became the belittlers denouncing the ridiculous notion of spirit all together. In the last century, the psychologist Dr. Carl Jung rediscovered the wisdom of the alchemical work and simultaneously, with his fascination with consciousness and spirit, he differentiated between two energies. The first one giving us access to our transcendent self, and the other responsible for the release of inner alchemy. Jung believed these two energies work creatively in the world. In fact, he speculated that together they create the world as we experience it.

Today quantum physics, a science that is gaining more and more respectability, agrees with this dual theory stating that matter and energy come together to create the experience we have of this universe.

I speculate that the womb is the tangible place where these two forces come together in our bodies. As a womb-carrying human you can give life to a human being, and even though we try to understand every biochemical, physical, and mechanical aspect of human procreation, we are still faced with the *miracle* of creation. We may know how the egg and the seed come together in a woman's womb. We may have discovered the chemistry that makes the mom go into labor to birth her baby. Yet, when it comes to how and why we are able to create and birth a life we still have more questions than answers. In fact, as a doula, I can tell you that the more births I attend the less I can predict what, when, and how a child will come into this world if the birth is left to the natural way of things. This very real concept of our womb being both a portal for the divine and a creator of life has inspired my concept of Uterus Mundi.

The Uterus Mundi is the chalice where we can place our dreams and desires, all those things we like to manifest into creation. Just as we nurture a new life from the zygote, to the fetus to a fully formed and able human, so we can cultivate a new expression of ourselves.

Combining the spiritual practice of self-awareness and the actual alchemy released as a result of our journey through the nine chakras of creation, we can use our womb to place the seeds of creation and bring to fruition that which we desire.

The Work Ahead

Being a womb-carrying human makes us precious, valuable, and a great asset to life itself—we must exist for men-kind to exist. Carlos Castaneda's *Don Juan* tells us that, *"The universe is female. Women have total access, they're already there…Women are portentous fliers; they have a second brain, an organ they can use for unimaginable flight. They use their wombs for dreaming."* Unfortunately, most women have experienced a violation of their sacred womb in some capacity, whether it was through the violence of non-consensual sex, through abortion or miscarriage, through a challenging birthing experience, taxing menopause or menses, or a hysterectomy. The womb is a creative chamber we can use for cultivating any seed/intention we place in it. To do so we need to heal our womb and begin to have a conversation with it daily.

The work ahead is laid out in nine steps, which correspond to the nine energy centers referred to as the *Nine Chakras of Creation*. In my years of studying and working with the chakras I developed a healing modality that can help us navigate the journey of knowing and reclaiming our womb power. The nine chakras are filters, lenses, and tools through which both past and present must travel in order for your future to manifest. The concept of chakras and energy centers dates back centuries and can be found in most philosophies and religious texts around the world. The wisdom of the chakra system is used in several healing modalities as gateways for healing and a deeper understanding of one's life purpose. Reiki masters work on energy blocks within chakras in the body with the intention of healing different aspects of people's lives. Traditional Chinese healing sciences, like Tai Chi, assert that the body has natural patterns of Chi energy associated with it, and illnesses are seen as the product of disrupted or unbalanced Chi movements within the chakra system. The science of Acupuncture recognizes the Chakras (Taiji Pole), as the main energy conduit in the body. Qi Gong is the Mandarin Chinese term for the Chakra System and states that Chi energy flows through energy channels known as meridians. Hindu mystics numbered the chakras in the body in the hundreds of thousands (this is very similar to the meridian system used in acupuncture and shiatsu therapies.)

The Nine Chakras of Creation are energy centers that correlate to *Nine Basic Human Rights* and mimic the birthing energy flowing from the heavens to the earth.

The Nine Chakras of Creation & Nine Basic Human Rights

First Chakra - The right to be here

In our first chakra we get in touch with our roots and our ancestral connection to the Uterus Mundi, playing on the concept Anima Mundi, which originated with Plato. Here we discover our intrinsic connection with all living things on the planet. We will acknowledge our families, our tribe, and heal the past to let go of all that was. We will learn how to nurture our roots, and strengthen our right to be here.

Second Chakra -The right to feel and the right to want

This is the physical cradle of the womb. It is the center of our creativity, and relationship with the other. Our self-esteem is deeply rooted here. We will come face to face with the womb's gifts and begin to heal its defilement. We will reaffirm our right to say no, to question perceived authority, to stand up for ourselves, and our sisters'/mothers'/daughters' rights to an un-violated womb.

Third Chakra - The right to act

The third chakra is considered the center of vitality, energy, willpower, action, and achievement. Here we will learn about taking actions of self-empowerment, self-understanding, and self-wisdom; we will explore the shadow energy used to seemingly protect you from love.

Fourth Chakra - The right to love and be loved

The fourth chakra is the energy of Venus, of self-love, and self-compassion, as well as love and compassion for others. We will understand our history of love and find the keys to opening our heart through vulnerability and using love as a healing tool.

Fifth Chakra - The right to speak the truth

This chakra is about honesty. Our soul carefully listens to our words and how they relate to our true intentions, as well as our actions. In the fifth chakra, you will learn how your words are your currency, and you will learn how to silence your chattering minds and listen to your intuition as though your life depended on it.

Sixth Chakra - The right to see and perceive the truth

The energy of the third eye leads us to wisdom and the realization that we create our own reality. Here we discover how we learn and process information. What we see and how we see ourselves is explored. We will embrace detachment with wisdom and compassion.

Seventh Chakra - The right to know

In your seventh chakra, you will deepen your practice of meditation and prayer, releasing control over to the Divine, trusting in its process and in the universal love for you. This is the portal through which the Divine mind comes into your body. Here you will meet the dweller at the threshold; here you will learn how to let the old die so that you make room for the new.

Eighth Chakra - The right to your Divine Power

Unencumbered by the weight of obstacles in all other chakras, this one affirms your right to your infinite Divine powers, showing you how to manifest what is yours by Divine right. Here we learn how to dance with our shadows, embracing and harnessing their power to allow our spiritual transformation. We will explore our psychic powers and our ability to see the future.

Ninth Chakra - The right to be one with the miraculous

In the ninth chakra, you become one with the Divine. The time has come, the tools have been learned, and clarity of intentions obtained. This is the time for gratitude and presence. Being one with the Creator requires integrity and inner wisdom. The circle completes and we come back into the Uterus Mundi. We are ready to give birth to a new self!

A Note About the Format

In this book you will find the tools through which both past and present must travel in order for your future to manifest. When you can finally place within your healed womb a new seed that is a new you, a new project or your heart's desires; when you are willing to do the work to care daily for the seed, nurture its growth, and feed its soil, then you will see it grow strong and healthy. Then you will have prepared your new self to be born effortlessly and painlessly.

You will be asked to write, think, and take your time. There are a lot of exercises that are designed specifically to help you follow a certain path to heal your womb and begin a lifelong conversation with it. Each part begins with a question. We recommend asking the question and letting go of all immediate answers. Let those questions resonate in your womb and rejoice at the messages you will receive, which may come at times in your dreams, as a whisper in your ears, or as a feeling on your skin. Regardless of how you feel in the moment, doing the exercises is quite important.

With that awareness I suggest you do not read ahead just because you do not feel like writing, or because you do not want to write on the book, or there is no paper or pen around. Attach some paper and a pen to this book. If you truly want to reap the benefits at the end of this journey, you get to take some time to write, even when it seems that nothing is coming up. I often give sample answers, but please don't give in and circle the one that seems most likely. The act of writing helps you clarify your thoughts, remember things better, and reach your goals more surely. Dr. Gail Matthews a psychology professor at the Dominican University of California found that people who wrote down their goals, shared them with others, and maintained accountability for their goals were 33% more likely to achieve them, versus those who just formulated goals. In *Write It Down, Make It Happen*, author Henriette Anne Klauser says, *"Writing triggers the RAS [reticular activating system], which in turn sends a signal to the cerebral cortex: 'Wake up! Pay attention! Don't miss this detail!' Once you write down a goal, your brain will be working overtime to see you get it, and will alert you to the signs and signals that […] were there all along."*

Make sure at times you rest; put the book down and come back when you are ready to write and explore the exercise. Remember that at the end of this book you will be given an exercise that uses your journal entries to find out your purpose in life.

PART I
The Womb

Could Our Womb Be A Creative Chamber to Manifest Anything We Desire?

Following the publication of my first book, *Painless Childbirth* in 2008, I began holding workshops all over the world using the self-discovery tool I call the *Nine Chakras of Creation*. An important lesson became clear from the very first seminar I ever offered: womb-carrying humans heal through feelings (specifically gut/womb feelings) and through both physical and emotional support from other women (spiritual midwives). To my delight women from around the world enrolled in my workshops bringing a wide variety of perspectives. There were younger women who were either pregnant or wanting to get pregnant, who longed to heal before conception, as well as older women who had never had children, couldn't carry a child to term, or were menopausal. There were those who had terrible birthing stories of abuse and unwanted medical interventions, and those who had repeated cesarean births and felt deprived and hurt by their memories. There were doulas and midwives, women's advocates, and therapists. Some were attracted by the concept of having a conversation with the part of their body that held physical or emotional pain. All of them shared a common desire to go on an inner journey to heal the self, discover and strengthen their life path supported by a group of loving women.

In these workshops, we spoke about listening to our inner voices and began the practice of having conversations with our wombs. First, we had to come together to define the qualities of our Divine Spirit and how we imagined a Celestial Mother would communicate with us. When it came time to distinguish the messages we were receiving, some pressing questions arose: *How do we discern the messages that come from our Divine, nurturing, and loving Spirit from those that come from logic and reason, yet are colored with judgment and/or reproach? In essence, how do we know if our gut feeling is something to follow or not?* To find these answers we began splitting the messages we received into two groups. We placed the voices that were harsh, belittling, and judgmental in one. Those that were far-out, but always exalting, loving, and caring were placed in the other.

We then noticed that for some participants the messages were neither harsh nor loving, but came through as a *to-do or not-to do* list. We began to experiment with detaching from the words and tuning only into the feelings experienced while hearing the messages. If our feelings were of a positive nature, we resolved that the messages must have been coming from Divine inspiration. On the other hand, if the messages made us feel ashamed, belittled, anxious, or overwhelmed we agreed that these messages were shadows coming from past negative belief systems. Let me give you an example:

One day a woman in her fifties was asking about her future direction and heard a message that said, "*dance.*" Immediately a sense of joy came upon her. Yet, almost concurrently, she heard another voice saying, "*You are too old for that; you cannot be a dancer at your age. You are making a fool of yourself. You cannot make a living doing that. You will hurt yourself doing that. What a silly idea!*"

Her conflict was obvious. Dancing seemed quite absurd as a future direction, and when she tuned into the judgmental, yet rational, messages she found them disheartening. At this point we suggested she let go of all the words and simply delve into the feeling that the action of *dancing* elicited. If the feeling was overwhelmingly positive, we decided that, regardless of logic, dance was the one thing she would do. The idea was that through dance she would be inspired to discover even more about her true path. She changed her daily practice from meditation and yoga to dance, and began having deep transformative conversations with herself. She was laughing hysterically at and with herself as she used her imagination to chase after her wildest dreams, allowing the sense of child-like wonder to come back into her life. She told us that one day, while dancing and spinning in a Sufi-like trance, she received a message. Here is her story:

> I was in my living room where I had removed some of the furniture so I could transform it into a dance floor whenever I wanted. My hardwood floor felt warm to the touch of my feet, and as I allowed the music to enter every cell of my body, I began spinning in place as I had seen the Sufi's dancers one night, long ago in Istanbul. I was transported in the interior of the Tekke (a Sufi convent) where a shady atmosphere and the soft music of a flute and tambourines embraced me.
>
> In the center of a circular hall, men clad in black and with long fez hats were bowing towards an elderly man with a white beard, seated with his back upright and his arms crossed. Slowly moving away, the Dervishes

formed a large circle, while the music slowly changed rhythm with the sound of the Turkish flute which filled the atmosphere with a melancholic and insistent cry. After a long meditative time, the Dervishes got up again forming a circle. Their movement was so slow and concentrated that I could hardly acknowledge that they had moved. Their expressions were so much out of this world that their eyes looked without seeing. It seemed like they were looking to the profundity of their own interior world, vividly aware of the moment, of themselves and of what surrounded them.

One by one they removed their black attire, perhaps symbolizing the separation from the ego. Their white tunics shined with splendor. These tunics were white garments with a long sleeveless robe, on top of which they had a short jacket that was tied at the waist. Slowly, raising the right arm towards the sky while the left arm pointed to the earth, the Dervishes began moving very slowly around one another and around the center.

As they continued circling, I found myself in the middle of their circle. At first I began feeling afraid, but soon I could feel the wind their garments were creating and began allowing such wind to inform me. I heard myself begin a conversation with the wind, *"I am here, I let go, I am ready."* A voice responded, *"Yes, you are and they know it, rejoice and spin as the Dervish do."* I kept spinning till I gently fell to the floor, and breathing deeply I knew somehow what my path would be. Shortly after this journey I went to research what I could about the Sufis and their practice and I learned that a Sufi's way of life is to love and be of service to people, deserting the ego and all illusion so that one can reach maturity and perfection, and finally reach Allah, the True, the Real. I resolved I'd find a way of being of service.

Today, she is not only a wonderful dancer who uses that medium to meditate, but is also a successful life coach and mentors teenaged women on their career path. Dance, and a willingness to listen to her inner voices, have completely changed her life.

How often do we get a glimpse at an exciting new idea and forget to nurture it as a seedling? Why do we commonly listen to the voices that are standing in the way of our heart's desires and want to bring us down? Following our feelings instead of logic will surprise us, and inspire us to think out-side-of-the-box, which can lead to a new direction in life. These new ideas are the seeds that grow into a new life purpose, a new path, or whatever you are ready to conceive.

The beliefs and experiences of our past create the judgmental voices that stand in the way of our faith. When doing this work the following questions also came up: how can we disinherit our family and tribe's legacies filled with judgment, fears, and pain, and at the same time harness the good from our past while being completely independent individuals? Can we find or improve the way we give and receive love and begin gentle conversations with ourselves that stir us in the direction of that love?

One woman who was concerned about her mother's cancer legacy asked, "Can we change a seemingly impossible task (our genetic makeup) and have the health and the body we want?" These are tough questions and, at times, it seems that the more questions one asks the more continue to surface. My suggestion is to create a daily practice of giving yourself the time and space to be quiet and listen to the answers and feelings that come.

During my workshops, I encourage women to choose the messages that feel good and jot them down in a journal. To gather them as seedlings to be planted in a fertile soil, a place far away from our intellect and all the seemingly logical reasoning of why we couldn't, shouldn't, and wouldn't do this or that. During this process of finding a safe place for our heart's desires, I came upon a realization: As women, we have a remarkable organ, the *womb*! It can literally birth a new human being! *What if we place our seedlings in our womb and let them grow from there? Could we use our womb every time we wanted to create something new in our lives? Is the womb the place where these voices come from, and is it the place where we can have these conversations?*

Excited by this revelation, we began deepening our understanding of our wombs. Here's a list of womb definitions from women all over the world.

+ Our womb brings forth life on all levels of body, mind, and spirit. Within it there is a healer, a counselor, a confidant, a sage, a decision-maker, and an artist.
+ Every face and facet of our being has roots in the womb, making the womb the logical domain for our healing process.
+ Our womb is our defining difference that gives us an advantage.

+ Our womb is the seat of our being, our first creative spark, the place of absolute Divine presence and power, a sacred space, a gateway, and portal.
+ Self-esteem and the womb are synonymous with one another.
+ The womb is the perfect chamber to contain and transform negative or harming energies, with our monthly blood we can strip away negativity.
+ The womb knows and understands the true essence of who we are born to be. It wishes for us to remember to connect with the Universal Mother. It rejoices in the eternal now of the Divine spirit.
+ The womb is the source of a woman's deepest strength.
+ The womb is not only the seat of physical creation, but also of our creative expression.
+ Ideas are born in our womb; it is our 'gut' feeling that tells us to do something, follow a particular intuition, change careers, or launch a new endeavor.
+ If our womb/self-esteem is not healed the idea might come, but the action will not.
+ Our womb yearns for healing love. It has known pain of various degrees. It knows that tender loving care is a catalyst for being made whole.

Inevitably, when we begin talking about our womb and what it means to us, sacred tears stream down our cheeks. A lot of sorrow often surfaces in this work, and it becomes clear that there is a need to heal the womb and the pain that is associated with it. We all need to begin listening and talking to our wombs. The time has come to take our womb's power back through healing and understanding its potentiality, as well as harnessing its ability to create and manifest the life we deserve and desire.

Our womb is the soul's physical cradle. From the moment menses began, your body has been calling your attention to this special place. It has been anointing you with the sacred blood that makes you who you are – a woman, creator, holder, and nurturer of our species. Your monthly rendezvous with your womb are designed to show you the phases of creation, nourishment, death, and regeneration, which mimic the life and death cycle of the entire universe. Your womb births children as well as your spiritual potential, personal healing, and the ability to relate at the deepest levels of intimacy.

Meeting the Womb as Young Women

Discovering the womb is an essential element of the healing journey for every woman. In essence, this discovery is like going back to our primordial home the one through which we were born and that hosted us as we became incarnate. Our mother's womb was the first place where we had a sense of what love is, where our first thought was formed, where our first dreams revealed themselves, and where our first fears developed. The womb represents the first loving embrace that we now seek throughout our lives. It was the place where we had no needs, and all our desires were fulfilled even before they became such. It takes a woman several years before she encounters her womb again. For some it happens as early as eight or nine years old, for others a bit later. Our womb announces itself through the sacred blood – the menstrual cycle. In fact, your life is based around your menstrual cycle whether you realize it or not. In today's Western culture, the onset of menstruation in young women has lost most of the luster it once carried. For decades it has no longer been considered as an experience to be celebrated or broadcast – just the opposite, in fact. Today, a young woman's first period is usually something very private, something she must hide, which is very unfortunate. Instead of celebrating soon after or slightly before your first conscious encounter with your womb through the first bleeding, many mothers give their growing daughters a warning. They remind them that, *"girls get pregnant"*; the cautionary words, *"you must be careful from now on,"* are added immediately, associating fear with one of the most important parts of being a woman. Many people today still overlook the first cycle as an important stage in a young girl's life to be celebrated. However, an increasing number of mothers are holding personalized menarche rituals, using music, flowers, jewelry, and dance to celebrate their daughter's entrance into womanhood.

Rituals are society's way of teaching and maintaining the culture. They are essential for restoring the matrilineal lines of initiation. A menarche ritual can make menstruation easier and more meaningful for both the young woman and her mother. Practicing rituals can be comforting during this delicate time and reminds a young woman that her feelings are natural and have been shared by other women throughout history. It focuses the attention of the community on the young women's needs and instructs her as to what her family and society expect of her as she is enters womanhood.

In several countries around the world, women have historically come together to cradle one another in times of need related to their wombs. Women in Judea were initiated into the Red Tent and sent to a Menstrual Hut or Moonlodge, during menstruation where girls were taught about their womb-powers, self-care, and how to care for each other. Navajo tribes commemorate a girl's first menstrual period with an elaborate four-day celebration called the Kinaalda. In this celebration the whole tribe participates in symbolic dances, cleansing rituals, physical activities such as racing, and enjoying a special cake called Alkaan. The festivities symbolize the physical and spiritual closeness to Mother Nature, as well as the literal transformation from a young woman to the image of Mother Nature. The Apache tribes have a similar celebration called the *Sunrise Ceremony* that consists of many matching activities and rituals that represent a young girl entering womanhood. Young girls are showered with attention during the four-day celebration, while other members of the tribe sing, pray, and dance almost non-stop. Through such rituals, these young women are not only given a renewed confidence, but a heightened sense of self as they receive significant recognition by the entire tribe.

There is magic inherent in the menstrual cycle. Each cycle provides a woman with the opportunity to understand and read the messages her body gives her for any specific healing she needs. Each cycle creates the potential for spiritual growth and personal development. All a woman has to do to connect with that potential is to simply be with her cycle each month and begin a deep relationship and conversation with her womb.

The distressing symptoms that so commonly surround a woman's menstrual cycle are often a result of ignoring the body's messages or symptoms. These messages indicate specific emotional and physical needs or imbalances. Our menstrual symptoms are usually "wake up calls" about the amount of toxins in our lives, whether from the food we eat, the company we keep, or the stress levels created from our lifestyle.

Here are some simple facts: The average menstrual cycle is congruent with the twenty-eight day lunar cycle. In the old days before the advent of electricity, women cycled with the moon. They ovulated when it was full, and bled when the moon was dark. From the pineal gland in our brain, messages are sent to our ovaries, via hormones, to release an egg based on the amount of light our brain senses in the night when we are asleep. At the point of most light, during the full moon, we are programmed to ovulate. Women who live in the countryside are more likely to be in sync with the moon, as are women living in tribal cultures. Ovulating during the full moon means bleeding during the dark of the moon, when the energy is more inwardly focused.

When you are not in alignment with the moon cycle, and have no idea what particular phase it is in, your cycle can be painful, irregular and feel like a huge burden. Women who begin regularly observing the moon, tracking its path across the sky, and noticing its waxing and waning, synchronize with the moon phases. Just like cycles of the moon, there are four phases (four weeks) within a menstrual cycle.

Week One (day 1-7) – first day of bleeding – This is the feminine quarter - It is the time to be quiet to listen and enter conversations with your womb. Go on a retreat stretch in bed, do light walking and yoga. It is not a good time to start anything new, and best to do a monthly review or life review. Listen in meditation while setting your intention for the coming month, metaphorically planting seeds for the new cycle. The fruit is harvested, the womb is cleared away through the sacred blood, so space can be made for a new beginning.

Week Two (day 8-14) – Preparation takes place in the womb, which is made ready to receive and accommodate the growth of a new life. This is a time for reasserting your values, setting your goals, and intentions. This is a great time to dance, play sports, and try new high-energy activities.

Week Three (day 15-21) – New and fresh life appears, and thus, the week of ovulation also carries the possibility of new life, through conception, or in the way of new thoughts and ideas. Here you may experience feelings of failure or elation depending on what you achieved from your creative peak in the few days after your egg has expired unfertilized. This is a great time to make love, salsa dance, tango, or anything that makes you feel sensual.

Week Four (day 22-28) – This is where the lessons from this cycle are seen and felt. Here we meet the dweller at the threshold (we'll speak about this figure in detail in the work ahead). We face our fears and are ready for the death-rebirth cycle. This is a perfect time to get your aggressions out through exercise like kick boxing, acro yoga, running, swimming, or surfing.

Recently, there has been an insurgence of interest and recognition in the sacredness of a woman's menses. Women are coming together in Red Tents to care for each other, bleed together, and explore their femininity. We know that those who live in close proximity to other women synchronize with one another.

Even scientists are now interested in the properties of menstrual blood. Modern medical research is now proving what ancient cultures have known for thousands of years: that menstrual blood has incredible healing properties, including the power to regenerate damaged parts of our body – previously deemed impossible. In 2013, the U.S. began its first successful FDA-approved trials using stem cells derived from menstrual blood to heal heart disease and blocked blood vessels.

Animal stem cells derived from menstrual blood have proven to be extremely successful in clearing blocked arteries. This is due to the powerful ability of menstrual blood stem cells to grow new blood vessels. Dr. Azra Bertrand, from Duke University, says, *"Perhaps the most amazing implication of this research is that the number of menstrual stem cells released by a single woman in one menstrual cycle could potentially be used to heal thousands of people."*

This is a new era in medicine and in consciousness. Womb-carrying humans have known for centuries the true power of the womb. It has been called the "Fountain of Life" or the "Fountain of Youth," but it seems most people have simply forgotten.

The Holy Grail, in its true original essence, is the womb. The power of renewal, rebirth, and resurrection previously associated with the Holy womb and menstrual blood of the Divine Mother was transferred to the story of Jesus and his ritual of Eucharist. "Hic est sanguis meus – this is the chalice of my blood." Worshipers 'drank his blood' to obtain rebirth through Him. In most ancient myths and religions, throughout the world dating back hundreds of thousands of years, the power of rebirth had always been a blessing of the Feminine Womb – embodied and gifted by the sacred womb priestesses across many cultures.

As we begin to remember our womb history and power, let's also restore the honor and respect that they deserve. By honoring our cycle we show respect for the feminine, the dark, the juicy, the mysterious, the science, the spirituality, the creativity, and sexuality of Mother Earth.

Conception and the Womb

When we conceive consciously, we experience not only the birth of a new life, but also the birth of a new self. Birth is another rite of passage, an experience that teaches us life-changing lessons about who we are, what we're capable of, and what we need to face in our lives to become mothers. During conception our womb is at its best, as it is fulfilling its life's purpose. The forty to forty-two weeks of gestation present another great opportunity to go on a journey of self-discovery as we develop a daily relationship with the new life that is growing inside our womb.

In my book, *Painless Childbirth*, I discussed how a mother's feelings influence the very DNA of the unborn child. I introduced the nine-steps methodology that can be used to manifest the desired birthing experience. Pregnancy is often the first time a woman experiences the miraculous. For many, pregnancy brings up spiritual questions like–*Where do we come from? Why are we here? Why do certain things happen?*

Pregnancy lures a woman inside herself. There is a necessary shift from the rational, left brain masculine approach to the creative, right brain feminine way. Pregnancy becomes an invitation into her inner world and a pathway to her spiritual journey. Instinctively, women are drawn to come together and learn from each other. There is a *Gentle Birth* movement unfurling its wings around the world helping women move away from the patriarchal model of maternity care and towards the ancient and nurturing midwifery model. In the last 30 years a new group of women—doulas—have surfaced to accompany women through this rite of passage with informational, emotional and physical support. I am one of those privileged doulas on a spiritual journey holding the sacred space for women to flourish during this time.

Women Coming Together to Care for Each Other

Once a woman has given birth to her baby, another important time ensues called postpartum or *mothering the mother*. This is another rite of passage, instrumental for the physical, emotional, and spiritual well being of the mother and child. In the immediate postpartum period it is important to create an open, quiet atmosphere of contemplation and reflection. All we need to do is look into our history throughout the ages to see that *mothering the mother* is a practice as ancient as birth itself.

In Guatemala and Mexico a postnatal woman is confined in what is called *la cuarentena* (quarantine) with her baby, and other women take care of her. They cook and clean and forbid her to work. In countries like Korea and China a specific period of postnatal confinement is also prescribed. These new mothers are served special foods and cared for by other women and are forbidden to do any type of work or heavy lifting. In India, henna is painted onto the feet of a woman after birth. A woman who has hennaed feet must let a friend or relative help her care for her older children, tend to the baby, cook, and clean. Haitian tradition dictates that new moms must be cared for as much as possible during their postnatal recovery period with plenty of warm baths and teas, daily massage and a period of confinement so that she can regain her energy after delivery. In rural Jamaica, the mother and baby go into seclusion for a minimum of nine days following birth. The midwife, grandmother, or nanny, cooks, cleans, does the shopping, chores, and takes care of the other children, as well as the new mother. They bathe and massage her, teach her the best nursing positions and how to bathe her baby. In our modern society this role, at times, is substituted by a postpartum doula.

Womb and Moonpause

Moonpause (or menopause), like menstruation and childbirth, is a portal into the sacred dimension of womanhood. Dr. Christiane Northrup says the peri-menopause is another labor, which results in a woman giving birth to a new self.

Menopause is known to bring up mixed feelings for a woman. This last rite is sadly never celebrated. In fact, many hide it in shame and fear of being seen as useless, old and unattractive. For many, menopause is a dramatic and fearful time. No longer fertile, a woman can either rejoice from the freedom of menopause or grieve at the loss of apparent usefulness in society. The wise crone, who was an instrumental figure when we lived in small villages, and was relied on for wisdom, fairness and counsel, has been forgotten in modern society.

In ancient cultures, menopausal women entered the doorway to become the wise ones, the grandmothers, the elders of the tribe or community. The wise woman's drum beats to a different rhythm. This is a fantastic time to reflect on your life and your past. It is a quiet time where you no longer need to achieve or nurture anyone one else, only yourself. For some of us, menopause means becoming a grandmother and having the great opportunity to see our daughters and sons become parents. We get to relive the beauty of seeing a young life blossom. The eyes of a grandmother watch from a different point of view. She is no longer 100% responsible for the well being of the new life, she can rest and indulge in simply loving and accepting them. She can offer her time and the patience she has learned in her life. She can slow down and play with the little ones and become young and playful again with her grandchildren. Having earned their respect she can become the confidant, the storyteller, the one who listens and does not judge. The menopausal goddess embodies the third aspect of the ancient triple goddess—the daughter or maiden, the mother or matron, and crone or wise-woman. Dr. Northrop tells us in her book *The Wisdom of Menopause* that during this time a woman has heightened wisdom and intuition.

I entered menopause at the age of fifty. That is also when I published my first book, began traveling alone around the world, and felt driven to design a tattoo symbol of the three aspects of the goddess – the maiden, the mother and the crone, which ended up on my right arm. This has been, and is, one of the best, and most prolific times of my life. My womb was drawn into intimate relationships as a maiden, filled with my children as a mother, and is now filled with ideas and creativity as a crone. It is said that once a woman has arrived here she can finally claim her wisdom. The journey of menopause must be honored and celebrated by all women. In many ways, it is a graduation, a crossing of the threshold into a new phase of life.

Womb Violations

There is no way we can talk about the womb without acknowledging the violations it receives physically, politically, spiritually and psychologically. In patriarchal societies, a woman's womb has been used to relegate women to the category of second-class citizens, and all its proclivities used as the explanation for women's inferiority.

For instance, did you know that the word hysteria comes from the Greek word *hystera*, meaning "womb"? The "*Wandering Uterus*" was a familiar term that went hand in hand with *Hysteria*. It was a belief in ancient Greece that a *wandering uterus* needed to be confined and controlled or it would cause a women health problems. In the past, healthcare providers were taught by the medical literati that women's constant mood swings and erratic behavior, which were referred to as *hysteria*, made them incontinent and unable to make rational decisions.

PMS, child bearing, and all the responsibilities and consequences of such womb power, have historically been used as mechanisms to keep women out of the work force when jobs were scarce for men due to the Depression or at the end of wars. Interestingly enough, in times when women were in demand in the workforce, research was used to demonstrate that PMS was not an issue and would not prevent them from being productive workers. To learn more fascinating history on this topic read Emily Martin's *The Woman in the Body: A Cultural Analysis of Reproduction*.

Research has shown that PMS symptoms are far more severe in women who are in, or have a history of, abusive relationships and are experiencing high levels of stress, feel overwhelmed at work, or are generally unhappy with their lives. This correlation suggests that women in these situations subconsciously inflict pain to their womb due to the suppressed frustration and rage they feel. Women feel the pressures of having to legitimize their position when competing in a male-dominated field such as business, adding to the stress that increases PMS symptoms.

Economic motives have been solidly at play when we take a look at medical assaults on our wombs. According to recent studies released by the World Health Organization, in the United States 36% of all babies were delivered via cesarean birth and nearly 60% of all births were either induced or augmented using a drug that creates a strong violent contraction in our womb to expel the baby. The same organization clearly states that a cesarean rate of 15% should be the norm.

As we embark on the second decade of the twenty-first century a number of medical, environmental, and social changes have profoundly affected human reproduction, depleting our wombs. About 6.1 million women, ages 15-44, have difficulty getting pregnant or staying pregnant, meaning that there are an increasing number of women turning to infertility specialists for help. According to a recent report by the Centers for Disease Control and Prevention, the number of deliveries using Assistive Reproductive Technologies (ART), like In Vitro Fertilization, nearly doubled between the years 2000 to 2009.

The U.S. Department of Health and Human Services declared that one of every three women has suffered a hysterectomy before the age of 60. Even though there is a general consensus among the medical community that most hysterectomies are unnecessary, this procedure has become the most commonly preformed gynecological surgery in the United States.

For decades, politicians have also been attacking our wombs as they continue to have heated debates over our right of choice when it comes to abortion (even factoring in pregnancies resulting from rape). When it comes to direct violence against women, the harsh fact is that every two minutes someone in the U.S. is sexually assaulted. Scarier yet, 54% of sexual assaults are not reported to the police. Regardless, whether we speak from personal experience or not, all of the assaults to women's wombs have consequently taken their toll on both men and women – culturally, spiritually, and socially.

Womb-Carrying Humans Fighting for Their Rights

All human beings have had to fight for their rights, and womb-carrying humans are fighting for very unique ones. In some cultures more than others the fight is still very challenging. Many of us are our own worst enemy in this fight. With low self-esteem in tow, women trample on their own rights by declining them, not demanding them, and not fighting for them. Not accidentally, the womb resides in the second chakra, the chakra of intuition and self-esteem. When a woman's self-esteem and intuition is wounded or abandoned their life becomes a result of external forces. Rather than being in command of one's own existence in a pro-active and empowering fashion, the modus operandi becomes reactionary and out of our control. It is common knowledge that people who fight for other people's rights but do not fully believe in their own cannot make a difference. How can a woman stand up for her right to something, let's say equal pay, if deep inside she doesn't feel like she deserves it in her own place of work?

Aside from the right for equal treatment and pay in the workspace, there are many more personal, subtle rights that are constantly challenged by our social, familial, cultural and religious environment. The right to speak and hear the truth, the right to love and be loved, the right to take action, and the right to know are just a few examples. If we are not taught to question authority as children, we might believe we cannot stand up for our rights to go against societal norms. This misguided belief can result in feeling compelled to consent to unnecessary medical interventions. Similarly, if we walk around with the belief that we are unlovable, we may not stand up for our right to be in loving relationships, overlooking the abusive patterns of our partner. If the right to voice our feelings of anger and frustration, or even joy and laughter, are denied in our childhood we might become incapable to stand up for ourselves or even believe we are deserving of any rights at all.

When any of these rights are out of balance, we observe that self-respect, fear of losing control, financial loss, ability to survive and thrive, and poorly balanced relationships are present. Eating issues such as anorexia and bulimia, along with buried emotions and depression, are associated with an unbalanced second chakra and an unbalanced womb. Unless you heal yourself you cannot heal the world around you or help another sister, mother, or daughter in need. When a woman identifies her patterns and learns how to let go of unwanted beliefs she is on her way to obtaining the life she deserves and desires. She is creating and cradling within her womb future generations of empowered human beings. Most of us living in the western world know this and understand the need women have to stand for their basic rights, but only a few of us have been given the tools to actually stand up for ourselves.

Much work needs to be done to re-write our history so that our reactions and actions stem from a positive and empowering place. Knowing this intellectually will not help. We must do the actual work. We begin by having an honest conversation with ourselves as we are the ones who are best equipped to heal what needs healing, and exalt into life our dreams and desires.

How To Start The Conversation

The *Nine Chakras of Creation* help us navigate through self-healing, and open the way for the Divine to become incarnate within our womb. Today, I realize that each chakra has within itself its own system of nine chakras. This is where *Conversation With the Womb* begins.

In the following pages, you will be asked some basic questions about who you are, how you feel about yourself and the basic rights you think you have. These nine steps are designed to help you do four things:

a. Identify your core beliefs.
b. Understand where your core beliefs come from and how they serve you today.
c. Shed those beliefs that no longer serve you.
d. Create new and empowering beliefs about yourself, your abilities, and your life.

By going through this process you will learn how to bring back into your life a sense of mystery, manifesting the magic that will unfold as you unfurl your creative wings. When women come together to help each other heal the womb, miracles happen and the next generation's well-being is preserved. Before we begin our womb healing work, I want you to create a little altar in your home. You can use a small table, a purse, or a box as your altar. At the end of each chapter/chakra you will be asked to place an object in your altar. This object will represent the seed of that chakra and will serve as a reminder of the work you've completed. For example, for the first chakra you could use a rock from your garden and write on it a word that represents an important lesson you have learned while doing the first chakra exercises. The object can be anything you want, as long as you associate it with a deep meaning. The intention is that by the end of the book your altar will be filled with objects that represent each individual chakra seed you have placed in your womb. The seeds will begin to grow as you cultivate your practice of the Nine Chakras of Creation and you nurture them to blossom and manifest.

PART II
Nine Chakras of Creation
and the
Nine Basic Human Rights

Chakra Qualities

Every single one of the Nine Chakras has an effect on your physical, mental, and emotional well-being. Subtle energy is always traveling within and around your entire system. Any weakness or exaggerated energy in the chakra will manifest itself in some way. These energy centers can either spin too fast or too slowly, which create detrimental physical symptoms followed by emotional imbalances and behaviors. You experience these symptoms occasionally or frequently, depending on the characteristic of your personality. A balanced chakra contains qualities from both fast and slow spinning energy. When in perfect balance this enhances your well-being, thoughts, actions and emotions.

As you read each chapter you will begin to recognize the qualities of the three states of your nine chakras. Before judging yourself harshly, it is important to realize that all characteristics, perceived as either good or bad, are indeed QUALITIES. A quality is an essential distinctive attribute of who we are. Instead of judging individual qualities, and ascribing blame or shame to them, we get to find out how to harness their energies, redirect them, and let them loose. Our shadows are part of us. They are our flip side. The Yin to our Yang, the Heads to our Tails. In order to identify these qualities we get to recognize movements of energy within the chakras.

The chakras express themselves in two ways, through our senses and the actions that result from them, and with the larger energy that is the source of all things. Thus, we experience the world both as an individual and as a part of the whole.

When you break up with somebody, where do you feel it? In your stomach, in your heart, in your gut, or caught in your throat? When you are intellectually overwhelmed does it feel as if your head is going to explode? Does it feel like you cannot unfurl your brow? These are the chakras communicating with you. Pay attention to these energy centers and intentionally begin to open and clear them.

Each chapter in this section will begin with a question to ask your womb. You can use this as a starting point for your journal entry. It will end with a closing prayer and a prompt to place on your altar an object that reminds you of the creative seed that will represent the result of the work you've done on that particular chakra. With this in mind, let us take an in-depth look at each of the nine chakras and the three states of energetic movement within them.

The Right to Be Here

Womb Conversation

*I pledge to listen and embrace the messages I receive
from my ancestors, trusting in my choice to be here
and my destiny to thrive in it. I am one with all of life
now and forever more. I am safe and all is well.*

Tell me what I can do to make you feel welcomed?

First Chakra – Being In This World

First Chakra - The Right to Be Here and to Thrive

The Root Chakra is located at the perineum between the anus and the sex organs. This chakra represents security, survival, and trust as well as one's relationship with possessions, society, and work. When we work on our first chakra we focus on our relationship with our lineage and ancestors by revisiting our entrance into this world. We uncover our hidden negative beliefs and turn them around to better serve us. The root chakra channels the earth's energy up to our higher chakra centers and helps us ground on the physical plane. It relates to how a person feels about their right to be here and there connection with their purpose. The more we ground ourselves and express gratitude for what is, the greater chance we have of realizing our dreams and developing into the person we are destined to become. When we lose our connection to the earth, we cut ourselves off from the healing source – Mother Earth.

Spins Fast: In Excess, Congestion, Disharmony

Physical aspects of the first chakra are heaviness, sleepiness, feelings of dullness, lethargy, tiredness, fatigue, and lifelessness. Emotionally, you will have frequent depression and sadness, which brings out behaviors such as insensitivity, laziness, hibernation, boredom, indifference, inability to relax, and quick mood swings. Common results associated with a fast-spinning first chakra are hoarding, difficulty letting go, being overtly materialistic, pessimism, greediness, selfishness, ambition, and exaggerated lust.

Spins Slow: Deficiency, Depletion, Disharmony

A slowly spinning first chakra is characterized by symptoms of cold feet, low body weight, weak knees, and difficulty with physical movements. Emotionally, you feel a sense of hopelessness, concern, absent-mindedness, and the feeling of being lost. People will often accuse you of being a daydreamer, suspicious, timid, uneasy, worried, disturbed, distressed, panicked, and prone to phobias. Your actions might be colored by second thoughts, indecision, exaggerated reactions, repression, suppression, insecurity, undisciplined behavior, restlessness, and disinterest. You have an overall sense that you do not belong.

Balanced – Spins Harmoniously

When the first chakra is in balance you experience self-mastery, high physical energy, grounding, and good health. As a result you are a careful thinker and good planner. You are family orientated and a tradition holder. Tradition holders are people who are risk averse, yet they can be highly competent in well-proven technologies and strategies, and occupy the role of protecting tradition.

By being conscious of your personal characteristics in each chakra you can find new gifts and activate the potential of your shadow energy. There is no need to condemn your negative characteristics. It is your choice. You can look at the characteristics of a fast and slow spinning chakra as negative traits or you can identify their innate qualities and repurpose them for your benefit. For example, the fast spinning first chakra's characteristics of greediness, selfishness, ambition, and a compulsive need to hoard, carry the innate qualities of a strong ability to save, to use caution, and to protect. This can be transformed into self-mastery, strong family ties, the ability to harness and preserve tradition, and good financial planning. In the physical realm, you can go from being unable to relax to channeling your restlessness into focused action with high physical energy. When it comes to a slow-spinning energy center, you can transform daydreaming into being a visionary and turn indecision into well thought-out actions.

Ancestry

In its infancy, human kind was first and foremost focused on survival. We depended on the tribe for our sustenance and safety. Similarly, a newborn child develops its first chakra characteristics from her relationship with her primary care takers. The work of the first chakra is based on these relationships. Some of us have had very difficult pasts and complicated dealings with our family of origin, which still color who we are, how we feel about ourselves, and what actions we take on a daily basis. We have sat on a therapist's couch recounting the terrible things done to us repeatedly, trying to understand why we are who we are. At times, many have felt a strong need to sever the connections with toxic family and/or tribe members. However, to simply let go of, or run from, your relationships and affiliations will not allow you to fully understand your purpose. While forgiving someone who has done something terribly wrong may not always be necessary, resisting the opportunity to learn from these hard life lessons will have real physical, emotional, and psychic consequences. This inevitably results in victim consciousness and accepting the notion that things "just happen" to us, i.e. "I had no choice and was just born into this family."

If we acknowledge instead the possibility that it was our choice to come into this world, and to learn these particular lessons with this specific family, tribe, and circumstances, then we can begin to experience a more empowered healing.

It Is Your Choice to be Here

The notion of a life before conception can be found in many religious texts, spiritual teachings, and oral traditions. Several Eastern and Western religions address the subject of life before conception hinting at reincarnation. Jesus refers to reincarnation in the following excerpt: *For all the prophets and the law have prophesied until John. And if you are willing to receive it, he is Elijah who was to come* (Matthew 11:13-14). *And, I say to you that Elijah has come already, and they did not know him. Then the disciples understood that he had spoken of John the Baptist* (Matthew 17:10-13).

By identifying Elijah, who was dead at the time of John the Baptist, Jesus is talking about his spirit coming back as another. Buddha himself, who preferred not to discuss God or the soul, still preached that what he called the "ever-changing individual character" moves from birth to another birth, until all changing and becoming comes to an end. In the Koran, we find the following excerpts: *And you were dead, and He brought you back to life. And He shall cause you to die, and shall bring you back to life, and in the end shall gather you unto Himself* (2:28). The Bhagavad-Gita states, *just as man discards worn out clothes, the soul discards worn out bodies and wears new ones* (2.22).

The notion that there is a life before life is a recurring theme in humankind's spiritual and religious belief systems. By accepting this notion, we come to understand that the decision of our coming into this world was not merely based on our parents' physical coming together, but a shared Divine choice *we* made with our parents. If we agree with the possibility that our right to be in this world is based on our own choice and embrace this idea, we can make peace with the world around us and investigate the purpose of this choice. However, before discovering this lesson it is necessary to observe and embrace your own birth experience.

Birth Memories – Embracing the Past

By learning our womb history as an un-born child we uncover the roots of the behaviors, mind-sets, and actions that baffle us. Studies have shown that strong events experienced in the womb can result in lifelong feelings of claustrophobia and hypochondria. Intolerable womb conditions can make the infant decide to be born earlier than normal. In adulthood this person might have feelings of not fitting in, impatience, and low self-esteem.

Some babies experience grief and loss once they leave the warm and cozy womb. Mothers who have had a traumatic birth feel grief at the loss of their ideal birth. Others, who lose a baby to a miscarriage, lose self-esteem as they feel unable to fulfill their role as women. Sometimes, as a consequence of our birthing experience, we find ourselves reacting to things, 'having our buttons easily pushed' by words or actions without knowing exactly why. We wake up angry or sad, unaware of the origins of those feelings.

To learn your womb history, imagine your mother as a laboring woman. What was it like for her to give birth to you?

Where you whisked away from her and placed in a nursery? Did she feel supported or abandoned? You might not know the answer to these questions or be able to ask her if she is no longer around. However, remember you were at your own birth! Stop right now, close your eyes and go back to being in your mother's womb. Imagine yourself as a baby and ask, *"How do I feel here floating in my mother's tummy?"* and *"How does it feel to be in labor and to be born?"* Take your time, close your eyes, and see yourself floating in the amniotic sac. Listen to the sounds that come to you, feel the emotions, and listen to the words all around you. Do you feel safe? Do you feel wanted? How do you feel about yourself? Take out your journal and write down any memories and feelings that come up. Are these feelings familiar to you? Can you tie them to any of your present day actions? You may begin finding associations between the feelings that came up during your birth experience and the feelings that currently drive you to take certain actions.

I have had clients who have remembered through hypnosis their painful experiences while in the womb and being born. One woman reported feeling that she had come into this world to save her teenage mom. Her mother's parents had kicked her out of the house due to her pregnancy. As a baby she took it upon herself to rescue her mother and was compelled to communicate the following message – *Don't worry mom. I will take care of you.* This resulted in a lifetime spent attempting to rescue everyone, even those who didn't want to be rescued. When this client came to my office she was depleted and experiencing postpartum anxiety. To help her, I proposed we use hypnosis to change her memories in the womb. After all, memories are fluid, they are not absolute, and are at our disposal to do with them as we wish. She came to me for several weeks and was able to travel back into the womb and let go of her need to rescue her mother. We brought her in to the memory of being an anxious growing child in her mother's womb. The adult-self then showed her child-self that her teenage mother actually ended up thriving and did not need to be rescued. I later suggested she share with her child-self all the wonderful things that she had accomplished in her life. Then we introduced her child-self to her newborn son, who expressed that he needed his mom to be present for him by letting go of the past. After weeks of this work and several sessions, she created healthy boundaries as we reinforced new memories. She called me one day completely elated, sharing that for the first time she had said no to a request she could not fulfill. This was her first step toward affirming her right to be here for herself, versus being here to help others.

Here is a short script that will guide you through an initial visualization of your birthing experience. Remember, it is always best go to a professional hypnotherapist to receive guidance. You can also find in-depth self-hypnosis tools and resources on my website www.joyinbirhting.com. I suggest using your computer or phone to record yourself reading the following script. Then find a comfortable quiet place to close your eyes and listen to the recording. Throughout the book, I recommend you do this every time you encounter a self-hypnosis passage. If you do not have a way of recording it, ask a good friend to read it to you so that you may get the full benefit:

> Take a deep breath in. And as you listen to my voice you are going to go deeper and deeper into a state of total relaxation. That's it. Now, envision your laboring mother, look at her with love and compassion, imagining as many details about your birth as you can. Look around. Where are you? Who is there with you? How do you feel? Imagine yourself

as your own mother's doula/midwife/partner. Support and encourage her. Take your time.

Now, witness her going through labor and your birth with you support. Speak to your baby-self. Bring her into your arms. Tell her how happy you are she has come into this world. Tell her that you love her. Tell her that she is wanted and has the right to be here. Take your time.

Now, imagine your grandmother as a laboring woman. See yourself as her doula for the birth of your mother. Welcome your mother into this world as you have welcomed yourself. Feel the love and the legacy of being wanted and having a right to be here. Take your time.

Go back as many generations as you can and ask each woman in your lineage for a symbol representing all of her love and wisdom. Now place each symbol as a seedling into your own womb. And gently imagine all the love and wisdom you have just received permeate into every cell of your body.

Now, at the count of three slowly come back into the room, back into your body, and open your eyes. One, two, three.

The entrance of a human being into this world creates an important shift in the universe, just like a drop falling into the ocean creates a wave that touches every shore. No drop in the ocean is less important, none is less impactful. Revisit this new memory as often as you wish making this your new birth story. You have the power to recreate your history, to change your memories, to insert yourself into the past, and heal the child that has suffered. Be compassionate and release any resentment you have about your own birth story. You can use this technique for any hurtful memories, as well as for the good ones. If your birth was a joyful, celebrated event, you can bring those good feelings with you into any dark place in your history where there is lingering pain. I call this, harnessing the light and shining it into the darkness. You are in charge and can be your own healer.

Questions on Hidden Beliefs That Come From Childhood

Now that you have had a glimpse at how your entrance into the world has influenced some of your behaviors, lets investigate the hidden beliefs that stem from your cultural, familial, and social upbringing during the first three years of your life. From zero to three years old you lived in your first chakra. Survival was your only task, yet you began to explore as you experienced the world through your close-knit tribe. You depended on your mother for everything and you focused only on your small nucleolus, your home, family and your parent's friends. The following questionnaire will shed some light on the hidden beliefs that you developed during this period, that are tied to your familial beliefs, which you have carried with you all your life. Once you identify them you will be given a chance to turn them around into positive affirmations. This is a sample of the types of questions you can use to distill the events of your life that have elicited strong reactions. By using these questions as a filter you will discover the primordial reasons for those reactions. Please fill in at least two beliefs in each category. Make sure to use the tone of a loving mother who addresses her daughter in a loving way when creating your affirmations. Take your time when answering each question. There is no rush.

1. What are the negative beliefs I have about myself that I have formed during my childhood? (Example: I am not good enough; I think I don't deserve to have what I desire.)

    _____

    _____

    _____

    Affirmation: (I am just as good as anyone else and I deserve all that belongs to me by Divine right.) _____

    _____

2. What are my beliefs about the role of a woman in a family and society? (Example: A woman is there to serve men and are not as important.) _____

    _____

    _____

    _____

    Affirmation: (My place in society is to be a creator and a nurturer. I am a womb-carrying being with the responsibility of caring the next generation of powerful and peaceful human beings.) _____

    _____

3. What are my beliefs about relationships? _____

    _____

    _____

    _____

    Affirmation: _____

4. Any other cultural negative beliefs I have inherited
    (moral, religious, work related): _____

    _____

    _____

    _____

    Affirmation: _____

Your beliefs are at the base of your behaviors and the reason why your life is the way it is. If you desire to change anything you must first change your beliefs. Think about it, if Steve Jobs grew up in a family where he was told that success can only come to those who graduate from college, and he truly believed it, he would have never achieved the success he had, nor would have Bill Gates or Steven Spielberg for that matter.

After we affirm our right to be here and we turn around our beliefs, we acknowledge the good.

Acknowledging the Good

The time has come to acknowledge what you have done in your life that has been a break from the norm of your cultural, social, and familial expectations. You will also acknowledge those things that you have pride in that relate directly to your tribal inheritance.

> List the actions you have taken in your life
> that were different from the "norm" or from
> your family/culture's norm.
>
> _____
>
> _____
>
> _____

What achievements are you grateful for that are directly related to your legacy and place of origin?

_____

_____

_____

By acknowledging your accomplishments you embrace two important elements that make up who you are today. Seeing how and when you had the power to differ from the norm allows you to affirm that you are an independent and powerful individual. By recognizing your accomplishments, which stem from you roots, you acknowledge your connection to your chosen tribe.

You Have The Right To Be Here - How To Glimpse At Your Purpose

The realization that we are individual beings who have chosen to be here with this particular family and culture gives us the opportunity to discover our ultimate purpose. What would it feel like if you lived your life with a strong sense of belonging? Take out your journal and finish the following sentences:

I belong in this world because _____

I belong in this relationship because _____

I belong at this job because _____

I belong in this body because _____

I belong in this family because _____

Meet M., a client who came to me for help with her fertility challenges. After giving birth to two girls she wanted to try again, hoping for a boy. This time she seemed unable to get pregnant. What stood in the way was not a medical condition, but an emotional one. Here is what she said about the above exercise:

> When I began doing this exercise my mind wanted to answer the questions by switching the words *belong to* with *deserve*. Did I deserve to be in this relationship, or to have this job, this life, etc.? It seemed that the concept of belonging was not part of my vocabulary. I was more concerned with deserving or not deserving something, as if that was the only measurement of my worthiness. After all, if I deserved to be in this or that situation it depended on me being a good person and an intelligent and capable woman, deserving what society or my boss would give me as a result of my performance. If I was good my reward would be to be accepted by my boss, my husband, and even my children. In essence, what I wanted was beside the point; my focus was on what they wanted of me.
>
> When the exercise kept insisting that I look at it from the point of view of belonging, something really switched inside me. Belonging was not something I deserved or not; belonging was a powerful feeling of standing in the knowledge that I could be the one who chose my path, my life, my relationships, and my job. Did I belong here out of choice or was I simply accepting what was given to me?

During our hypnosis work on this feeling of belonging, my first recollection was the sense I had growing up with, that I did not belong in this world. My dad had really wanted a boy and not a girl as his first child. I even went back further, remembering the feeling of fear my mom had while I was in her womb, worried that she might be carrying a girl and the possible consequences she'd have to suffer because of it.

Once born, I recall doing everything in my power to deserve my father's love and acceptance, being the tomboy he wanted me to be, despising girls and all girly things as silly and inferior. I learned quickly that any strong emotions where not tolerated, and tears where just a sign of weakness frowned upon or worse – ridiculed. I also realized that I had chosen my husband accordingly, choosing a writer/artist who was willing to be a stay-at-home dad, in essence a wife, and that I had even chosen my career (law) to follow a non-feminine path. I was just what my father wanted – the breadwinner. I recalled how when I was in labor with my daughter, I immediately asked for pain relief at the hospital so I could keep in touch with my office buddies via text messaging. We were in the midst of an important case and I didn't want to miss out on anything.

During the session, for the very first time that I could recall, I burst out in tears. They were deep excruciating sobs that were also quite liberating. I truly did not feel like I belonged anywhere and certainly had no sense of what I really wanted. What was my purpose if not to please my father? Did I have a right to want something different than what I had? Gladly, you suggested I make no immediate and life-altering changes, but give myself time to heal my memories and ask myself some deep investigative questions in order to find my purpose and place it, as if it were a seed, into my womb to grow. I also realized that this pregnancy I longed for, was about once again, appeasing my father and giving him a boy as a grandson, and somehow my body was refusing to yield yet again. Now, I am not sure that the purpose of coming to you was about getting pregnant and having a son. Rather, I see it as finally finding my way to discovering who I am and what I want and, most importantly, where I belong.

Connecting to Mother Nature

By healing our first chakra we embrace the concept of *Uterus Mundi*, one single visible living entity containing all other living entities, which by their nature are all related. This is the place where all things come from, the Divine chalice that creates all new life. By connecting to this source you can be endowed with all its powerful creative energy and use it as your propeller into your manifested future.

I offer you a visualization that will help you ground and connect you through deep roots to Mother Earth as you feel the gratitude energy of mother and daughter flushing back and forth from the source. Find a confortable place where you are not going to be disturbed for the next fifteen minutes, lie down and close your eyes.

> Take a deep breath in and relax every muscle in your body from the tip of your toes all the way up to the crown of you head. Now, imagine sprouting small roots from every inch of your body shooting deep into the center of Mother Earth. That's it. Take your time. Feel yourself deeply grounded into the soil as a tree. Feel the earth nurturing every part of your body, informing you of its wisdom. You are not alone; feel your connection to Mother Earth herself.
>
> Now, imagine that a larger, stronger root develops right from your yoni and penetrates deep into the hot center of the earth. Feel this energy and see it traveling back up through your root and filling your chalice with immense gratitude. Mother and daughter rejoicing and acknowledging one another's existence. Do this every time you feel disconnected from your roots, your origins, and your purpose.

Now it is time to place your root chakra seed on your altar and nurture it with this prayer.

> ### Closing Prayer
> *I feel the warm earth beneath my feet. I feel anchored to the earth through my first chakra. I feel the warm red color of earth as it penetrates*

my body and flows down through my legs and into my feet, supporting me to move upon it. I make peace with the past and let go of all that does not serve me. I embrace and harness my uniqueness that comes directly from my ancestral lineage. I feel the richness of my history and I am grateful for the lessons learned.

The Right to Feel

Womb Conversation

I am grateful for every gift you have given me. I recognize your feelings and I pledge to listen to your messages. I acknowledge you as the seat of creation for everything I want, and everything I have.

How can I be of service?

Second Chakra –
Emotions Toward the "Other"

Second Chakra - The Right to Feel

The second chakra is located below your navel and above your pubic bone, right in the space where the uterus lays. It is often called the body chakra because it is where you connect with the physical body through your feelings. The second chakra is like a magnet that attracts and reaches for the *other*, sexually and emotionally. It is in the second chakra that we first discover our right to our feelings. So many of us were born to families who denied our feelings, whether it was a conscious or unconscious act by our primary caretakers. We've grown in a society that tells children to be seen and not heard, where a crying baby is told to stop crying, a laughing child is quieted by a busy distracted adult and a teenager is belittled and told she is hormonal and being dramatic. It starts from the very first expression, when a baby is born it often comes into her mother's chest crying, and we are quick to shush her and tell her, "Don't cry...it is ok." In essence, we're telling her that whatever she is feeling, in the very moment she has taken her first breath, is not valid. I often suggest to my clients to change that first message to a welcoming message, something like "Wow, is that your voice?

How lovely, tell me more." But, most of us did not have that privilege. Historically women have always had to fight for the right to express their feelings. The right to have our feelings is so important and it is not a coincidence that this right is attached to the chakra where our womb resides.

All life/creativity/purpose begins in the second chakra, the seat of the womb. There was a time when our ancestors recognized the womb as sacred. In these times the womb was honored with titles such as the vessel of new life, the channel of the Divine, and creative energy. As we begin a conversation with our womb we explore our connection with God and the many stages of our relationship with this divine organ.

Spins Fast: In Excess, Congestion, Disharmony

A fast-spinning second chakra creates the perfect opportunity to attract a lot of drama and emotions into our lives. To numb our feelings we allow the incessant chatter of our minds to distract us from our emotions. Many times a fast-spinning second chakra correlates with sexual addictions, obsessive attractions, and a wild and un-parented inner child. Congestion in this energy center can lead to exhibiting poor boundaries, feeling a great deal of possessive energy, jealousy, and even the attempt to appease the emptiness in our womb with an unjustified need to have more stuff and to hoard. The digestive organs of the large intestine, the bladder, and the appendix are the anatomical parts controlled by this chakra; as well as the skeletal areas of the pelvis, the hip, and also the lower vertebrae. A spinning fast chakra will have lots of inflammation in these areas.

Spins Slow: Deficiency, Depletion, Disharmony

People with a blocked second chakra are usually very hard on themselves, inhabiting feelings of guilt and blame, which can lead to feelings of isolation and withdrawal from life. They experience frozen sexual energies, impotence, and lack of vitality. Emotionally, they are often aloof and inflexible. The chance of them experiencing emotional numbness is high. They grieve and feel guilty without even knowing why they are grieving. Physically, they experience digestive disorders, problems with their uterus (difficult menses, challenging menopause, violent childbirth), and they may be prone to bladder and kidney stones, or experience sciatica flare-ups.

Balanced: Spins Harmoniously

The characteristics of a balanced womb chakra are spontaneity, harmony between higher, middle and the lower self, trust in self and a healthy sexuality. People with a balanced second chakra live a non-judgmental existence and can express and attract richness in feelings and relationships. Many who are lead by this chakra are artists and creators of music and beauty. When you turn around some of the fast and slow acting shadows of this chakra you can use your tendency of being too hard on yourself and translate it into a desire to improve yourself. As you unblock the lower hips of a slow spinning chakra you can become a great dancer and mover. The exceeding sexual desires of a fast spinning chakra can transform you into a great and generous lover. A harmonious second chakra will turn your aloofness into expansion, your judgments into discernment, and your possessiveness into the ability to detach with love.

The Womb and God

> *"Before I formed you in the womb I knew you,*
> *and before you were born I consecrated you;*
> *I appointed you a prophet to the nations."*
> Jeremiah 1:4 -5

Since mothering is our first proverbial template for an existence in which we feel welcomed or rejected, loved or abandoned, many of us fuse our relationship with our mothers to our concept of God. A study shows that children's sense of God's closeness is related not to their mother's religiosity, but to their mother's attachment style, meaning whether the mother is calm and confident in her relationships, or anxious and uncertain. Many studies have now confirmed that how babies cope and make decisions in the womb can and will affect the rest of their lives.

Our relationship with the womb began as either a welcoming heaven or a dark unwelcoming unknown. Your mother's relationship with her own womb was automatically passed on to you. In her womb you lived a symbiotic life and you felt and absorbed all her fears, anxieties and grief, joys and excitement, her spiritual connection, and love (or lack thereof) for her partner.

At a recent workshop a woman told me that she remembered feeling tremendous grief from leaving the comfortable and cuddling feeling of her mother's womb. It reminded me that even if your life in the womb was wonderful the loss of this perfect and safe environment could create lingering grief.

A newborn can also experience grief due to early separation from the mother and/or harsh conditions in the delivery room such as noise, blinding light and cold temperature.

Unfortunately, many babies who are born in hospitals are still taken away from their mothers and left alone to cry while being checked by the doctor and nurses, especially during a cesarean birth.

Dr. Harville Hendrix, an educator and therapist known for his techniques on couple's therapy, spoke in his book, *Getting the Love You Want*, of our human yearning for Divine union. He defined this as a desire to return to a moment in our life when we did experience the perfect union. It's a period of time all of us experienced when we were one with the universe, when all our needs were met and we felt completely safe and secure. He speaks of the first nine months of our existence in the womb as the foundation for our lifelong urge for union with God. Hendrix would say that this urge is really a longing for the peace and tranquility experienced in our mother's belly.

Since all of us have experienced a life in the womb, and many of us lived through one or more traumas while in it or from our separation from it, it follows that grief is held in the second chakra where it was first experienced. In fact, much of the grief experienced later in life is transferred to this chakra (our feeling chakra) until the path is cleared and the tools to heal have been integrated.

Meeting Your Womb for the First Time

A woman's intuition comes directly from her gut. The gut is the place where the womb lives and we meet our wombs over and over again several times in our lives. When I was only nine years old I got my first period. It was a shameful time for me. My mom left the room and, without telling me, called my dad who announced it to the world. No one had told me what to expect and I remember at first being scared and then deeply ashamed. As a mother I made sure I told my daughter early enough what to expect and how important this rite of passage is for all women. She called me one day from a party and was freaking out because she was bleeding. I told her all was well and that I would pick her up immediately. I asked her what she felt like doing and she requested we go to one of her favorite restaurants. She ordered a chocolate malt and as she sipped the delicious drink, and looked at me with big scary eyes, I explained to her what this meant and that this would happen every month from now on. I remembered asking if she wanted to celebrate or do something special for it. At 12, she preferred to keep it private. It hurt a bit, as I wanted to reclaim my own rite through her. But, recognizing this was her moment, not mine, I respected her choice.

Underneath the color of our skin, all women bleed the same, red, deep, primordial flow of life force. This is the first time we all meet our womb. A woman's blood is often considered taboo – uncomfortable to many including women. There is a lot of stigma around a woman's moon cycle.

Somehow, even despite our knowledge, we are conditioned from birth to think of our periods as punishment for being women and give in to the notion that we stain the world with our blood. Sometimes, daughters aren't the only ones experiencing a myriad of feelings from their first period. Much like I did when my daughter refused a celebration, some mothers feel sadness during this transitional time. Whether it comes from an attempt at reclaiming one's own rite of passage or merely from recognizing the approaching next phases in a mother's life, the conditioning we get from our society around this transition is bound to bring out all sorts of emotions.

The menarche (our first blood) is an initiation into womanhood, a rite of passage lost to modern culture. Regardless of your past experience, consider creating a ceremony that properly acknowledges this transition while also honoring the excitement of your little girl becoming woman. The beauty of this work is that it is never too late to perform an initiation ritual. This is something a mother can do with her daughter or a woman can do with her friends. Even if you are already going through menopause, or if you have had a hysterectomy, your body knows; it has memories that still need healing. It saddens me to hear a woman speak of her own blood as a hindrance, without awe or respect. And yet, I understand the pain and its emotional source. When the blood that could have nurtured a life is lost as it flows through us, we may experience pain as a primal feeling of loss for the life that didn't become. Some women mourn each month at the lost chance of becoming a mother. This may sound irrational, yet it is our natural instinct that drives our need to procreate.

Resist the urge to think of your periods as messy or dirty. Would you consider a forest to be dirty, or the great ocean floor to be messy? In the modern world, a woman's period is designed to feel cumbersome and out of place. Through the meticulous drive of colonization the sacredness of this moment has been beaten down. Yet, despite the internalized drive to suppress the very things that connect us to our animalistic nature, menstrual blood persists as a life giving and cosmic force. We bleed to the rhythm of the moon. There is great power in our blood. Since the ancient times women's ability to bleed from their womb was considered sacred, powerful, and magical. It is only through shame that the wisdom and power of a woman's body is robbed of its sacredness.

Bleeding involves depletion essential for restoration. It is a process of self-regeneration. In our fast paced western culture women have to work at the same speed as men who do not have this organic life-regenerating mechanism. The fact that women need to rest during their cycle does not demonstrate weakness.

In fact, it speaks of wisdom. A life without pause and rest can lead to shallow life experiences and burnout.

Women are naturally more in tune with the rhythms of nature since our bodies' sexual systems work in cycles. Once a month we bleed, sometimes in unison with each other when we commune together – a lost art that is being revived today. When we menstruate, our blood leaves our bodies to return to the earth. Nowadays, so many women have bought into the sterilization of menses that they skip the important step of returning the life-giving energy back to the earth. Their blood, as well as the many products marketed to keep this portion of the cycle "clean," end up in a landfill. However, there are many sustainable ways of completing a woman's cycle that bring her back to direct communication with the pulse of the earth.

To honor the cycles through which our bodies operate you can place your blood directly into the earth. Some women gather it in a diva cup so they can actually place it in a jar and nurture their plants. Other women are fortunate to have partners that appreciate its taste and have no qualms ingesting it to truly communicate soul-to-soul. Create or search for a red-tent movement near you and join, or organize a moon cycle. Women need other women to grow. We need spiritual midwives to chaperon us through what Carlos Castaneda called the "perceiving box."

> Don Juan called the womb the perceiving box. He was as convinced as the other sorcerers of his lineage that the uterus and ovaries, if they are pulled out of the reproductive cycle, can become tools of perception, and become indeed the epicenter of evolution. Evolution, in the case of the womb, was, for them, the awakening and full exploitation of the womb's capacity to process

*direct knowledge – that is to say, the possibility
of apprehending sensory data and interpreting
it directly, without the aid of the processes of
interpretation with which we are familiar.*

Sexuality and Spirituality

After we meet our womb and recognize the power and the
lessons within our cycle, our next relationship comes through
our sexuality. Sexual energy is the primal and creative energy
of the universe. All living beings are a product of sexuality, yet
the topic of sex draws a negative stigma. No matter the gender,
everyone has his or her own understanding and opinion of sex
and often sexuality and spiritually are considered diametrically
opposed.

Sexuality can be a vehicle into spirituality rather than an
obstacle to it. One of the most magical ways to express your
desire to be reunited with God is by merging with another
person through sharing your sexuality. The more deeply you
feel the longing to return to the womb/home, the more deeply
you may want to free your sexual nature.

When focused properly, the gift of sexuality can be a
profound modality for the ecstatic affirmation of human love.
Instead of attaching ourselves to any cultural/religious model
that places sex and Spirit as opposing forces, why not include
sex and God in the same breath? When we break free from all
forms of sexual conditioning what is human and what is Divine
become partners and sexual love is the bond that unites them
both.

Two activities that challenge the ego structure down to
its very core are meditation and sexual expression. Sexual
expression can be frightening. Meditation can be daunting.
Both require letting go of the negative mind's usual control. In

meditation and in sex, in order to become the master of your mind, you must escape from the traps that keep you absorbed at the level of thought.

> *"Holding the hand of your woman or man, why not sit silently? Why not close your eyes and feel? Feel the presence of the other, enter into the presence of the other, let the other's presence enter into you; vibrate together, sway together; if suddenly a great energy possesses you, dance together – and you will reach to such orgasmic peaks of joy as you have never known before. Those orgasmic peaks have nothing to do with sex, in fact they have much to do with silence.*
>
> *"And if you can also manage to become meditative in your sex life, if you can be silent while making love, in a kind of dance, you will be surprised. You have a built-in process to take you to the farthest shore."* Osho, *The Book of Wisdom*, Talk #7

Sometimes we confuse sex with love, but sex is not love. In fact, sex can be self-loathing. This is not a moral judgment of sex. You can do whatever you chose to do as long as you go into it with open eyes and take it for what it really is. Regardless of your intentions, or of the perceived need for release, you are sharing your energy with another human being and are compelled to undermine yourself when sex is done just for a physical release. Sex constructed for sexual release only is mutual masturbation with undetermined consequences.

If you do not truly know the other person, then you cannot know what energies you are taking on as a result of having sex. Sexual arousal and sexual stimulation are two completely different beasts. Sexual stimulation does not require love, it does not require knowledge, and it hardly even requires the other person for whom you have generated your stimulation. On the other hand, sexual arousal is an act unto itself that does not necessarily seek or need an outcome or "fulfillment." When sexual arousal is present, unless your heart is in agreement with your genitals (meaning unless the arousal itself calls for further action), often the act of arousal is complete without the need to demonstrate some sort of pre-determined sexual involvement. Sexuality can be the doorway to bliss or simply a night of debauchery that leaves you with a hangover, the consequences of which can result in much more than a day spent in bed. This is not to say that you must be married or in a committed relationship to have sex with another. This is just a reminder that every action we take, whether it is consciously or unconsciously chosen, has a specific effect in the body. As womb-carrying individuals, theses effects literally collect in the chalice that is our second chakra. During sexuality we receive, and hold energy, therefore we must be in charge of what we welcome inside our body. Our energy can either be depleted or nurtured; love, affection, clarity of intentions are nurturing factors; abandonment, disrespect can only leave you vampirized. With this awareness, remember to ask yourself if the energy being mixed with your own is in alignment with self-love and self-care. When sexuality is seen as a portal to spirituality, we allow the Divine to come through us. Using orgasms as the welcoming of the divine energy produced by two souls coming together in love and intimacy allows for creative energy to manifest.

Orgasms are powerful! Women can have multiple orgasms from different parts of their genitals, the deepest of which come directly from our womb. Next time you come together with a loved one, imagine realizing miracles while you are releasing in orgasm. Through this portal from a higher state of consciousness you are so much more open to receiving all the good from the universe directly. The kind of energy you welcome in is completely up to you. What you envision at the moment of orgasm can plants a seed within your womb that can either grow into a new idea, a new you, or into an energy that needs purging. In some religions and cultures men are encouraged to call forth their child at the moment of orgasm, recognizing the powerful meeting of Spirit and Sexuality. The same can be done through calling forth that which you desire. At the point of climax affirm what you want to manifest and use this powerful emotional, physical, and spiritual climax to bring it into life.

To ignore the erotic is to separate yourself from your originating force, and to squander this creative opportunity. Next time you are with a loved one take this opportunity to call forth your heart's desire and see what unfolds. Being aligned in all areas of your life provides you with a deep understanding of yourself.

Grief in the Womb

When working on our second chakra we get to recognize the importance of healing any traumas and grief deeply seated in our own womb, and in the collective womb of all women. Womb grief can come from violations through sexual violence, the loss of our desired birthing experience, the loss of a loved one (which includes losing a child via miscarriage), or the inability to procreate. Later in life, many women experience grief from the loss of their uterus due to a hysterectomy, or the common feeling of uselessness when entering menopause.

Grief and fear are synonymous of one another. Of the many obstacles that stand in the way of a new beginning, or a new life, fear is one of the most significant. How do we tackle this seemingly impossible task of relinquishing our fears? Time is the greatest healer when it comes to healing the loss of somebody or something that happened in our adult life, but what about the fear and grief that is ingrained in our personal history? Often we are unaware of these types of fears at a conscious level. Again, resist the urge to indulge in feeling overwhelmed and take heart in the following famous dictum: *"The pain I might feel by remembering can't be any worse then the pain I feel by knowing and not remembering."*

Psychologists tell us that awareness itself can begin the healing process. So many people go into denial to protect themselves from a loss, but to hide behind forced ignorance is like pretending a gash on your foot does not exist, yet expecting it to heal on its own. The first step towards healing is indeed becoming aware of the need to heal. Once we are aware, we need practical tools to help us manage not only the loss but also whatever else comes our way in the future. To refuse healing might result in finding ourselves stuck in grief, dissatisfaction, anger, and even depression.

In the face of great pain one's faith and beliefs face challenges. A bereaved person reassesses their spiritual definitions. Although we commonly focus on the emotional response to loss, it also has important physical and spiritual consequences to observe. Many studies have looked at the bereaved in terms of increased risks for stress-related illnesses. Colin Murray Parkes, in the 1960s and 1970s in England, noted increased doctor visits, with symptoms such as abdominal pain (grief in the womb), breathing difficulties (heart chakra depletion – loss of love), and insomnia (distortion of the eighth chakra, the chakra of dreams) to name a few. These visits happened in the first six months following a major loss. The five stages of grief introduced by well-known American Psychiatrist Kübler-Ross are as follows:

- *Denial* - Life makes no sense. We are in a state of shock and denial. We go numb.
- *Anger* - Anger can be directed to others, ourselves, and even God. Anger fuels your life, giving temporary structure to the emptiness you feel.
- *Bargaining* - After a loss, bargaining may take the form of a temporary truce.
- *Depression* - Empty feelings present themselves and grief enters our lives on a deeper level, deeper than we ever imagined.
- *Acceptance* - This stage is about accepting reality and the recognition that this new reality is permanent.

Another stage of grief, which absolutely comes before acceptance, was introduced by Melody Beattie in a recent talk I had the pleasure of attending. She calls this stage *obsession*. People who have experienced loss can experience obsessive, recurring flashbacks or nightmares, or obsessive negative self-talk. They cannot stop thinking about what happened and as a result they relive the loss repeatedly and the self-blame that accompanies it. Some join support groups, which are a good way to cope, but these groups have the potential to feed the obsession of needing or wanting to talk, as the bereaved relives the experience over and over again, and becomes addicted to this cycle.

A lesser-known definition of the stages of grief is described by Dr. Roberta Temes in the book, *Living With an Empty*

Chair - A Guide Through Grief. Temes describes three particular types of behavior exhibited by those suffering from grief and loss:

1. Numbness (mechanical functioning and social isolation)
2. Disorganization (intensely painful feelings of loss)
3. Reorganization (re-entry into a more 'normal' social life)

In reading these different theories on grief it is plain to see that the concepts put forth by both Kubler-Ross and Temes indicate that through the recognition and awareness of the varying stages of grief *reorganization and acceptance* are inevitable outcomes. Awareness of these stages is certainly a great remedy, and time is the great equalizer. Yet, there is one thing that these theories have not addressed, particularly for those who have experienced grief in the womb (or at birth) whose memories are deeply embedded in their subconscious.

Dr. Arthur Janov, author of *Primal Man: The New Consciousness*, has been telling us since early 1975 that, "*Painful things happen to nearly all of us early in life that get imprinted in all of our systems which carry the memory forward making our lives miserable.*" Hypnosis is a powerful tool that can give us access to these memories, re-live them, and integrate them in the present. This work can create a new way of living that does not spring from our past. This new way of living is what we are after and it comes from a newly healed self.

Altering a memory during hypnosis creates an updated memory that replaces the old one. Michael M. Merzenich, professor emeritus of neuroscience at the University of California, San Francisco, tells us that the brain is not an inanimate vessel that can be filled. It is more like a living organism with an appetite, one that can grow and change itself with proper nourishment and *exercise*. Thus, with the right tools we can heal the past by working diligently on redesigning not only our painful memories, but also our thoughts and feelings toward them.

The latest research in this field is based on a radical rethinking of how memories are stored in the brain. Scientists used to believe memories were like snapshots in which the details are fixed once they're recorded. Today, many experts accept the view that memories are stored like individual files on a shelf. Each time they are pulled down for viewing, they can be altered before being put back into storage.

No matter what kind of grief you are experiencing the following method for accelerated healing involves working with timelines. This exercise is very simple and extremely effective for changing patterns in the subconscious. All that you need to do is go back in your imagination (in fact, you can go back even before your birth). Visualize yourself moving through your life and engage your emotions as you recall the past. Stop when you reach a negative memory and slowly visualize it in detail. Recall it as if you were watching a movie or a TV show. Don't dwell on the feelings as they can take you to a familiar powerless state. Instead, watch the feelings pass through you with neutrality. Now freeze-frame on the particularly difficult scene and change the memory. You can add a compassionate person to it, someone who can protect the person in the memory. This could be your adult self if the memory is from childhood. Another way to heal the memory is by making peace with the events, people, and places in it. For instance, if the grief comes from the womb because you did not feel wanted by your mother, imagine that you can feel compassion for her knowing that she did the best she could under the circumstances. Imagine your adult-self loving your unborn-self unconditionally, reassuring that you're welcome into this world.

Here is a step-by-step exercise to assist you:

1. Go to a memory you feel is still lingering in your consciousness. Try the last fight you had with a significant person in your life.
2. Go back into the memory and start to change various aspects of it. Change the colors in the scene, the way people are interacting with you, or whatever else will be helpful, so that much of the emotions are taken away.
3. Look at the person you are angry with and study them, seeing them as a little kid who is filled with feelings that might not have anything to do with you.
4. Take a snap shot of the scene.
5. Study the person again and mentally ask them questions. How are they feeling? Did something happen to them to make them feel this way?
6. Ask yourself if there was something that made you feel this way, even before the incident? Was something said that pushed an ancient button that had nothing to do with the situation at hand? Did something engage a core belief like, "I am not good enough, or not worthy?"
7. Now ask yourself why are you still hanging on to this?
8. Imagine all this memory on a movie screen and make the screen smaller and smaller. Tap yourself on the forehead, gently with two fingers. Do this several times; tapping yourself each time the screen gets smaller and smaller until it disappears.
9. Now, replay the scene again and notice the changes in yourself and the way you feel. Are you still as angry? Are you still right?

As you work with the above process, replacing the blueprint held in your subconscious mind, you are causing the cells and tissues in your body and brain to form according to a new healthy pattern.

You will get faster results if you repeat this process a number of times. You are impressing new memories and new experiences in your subconscious. It doesn't matter how accurate or detailed your imagery is, but rather how much you are able to create the feeling of harmony. If you are new to using self-hypnosis it may take you a little longer to get the results; persistence is your greatest ally. You may want to work with a professional hypnotherapist or learn self-hypnosis with the help of guided audio recordings. Following this deep restructuring of your personal history you may find feelings of being overwhelmed with emotions. These feelings are the last vestige of your history influencing your present.

Manifesting with Feelings

Many great philosophers, motivational speakers, and preachers talk about how *your life is shaped by your mind. They say: change your thoughts and you will change your life.* I am going to offer a different approach. I believe that your life is shaped by your feelings. If you have good feelings about who you are, what you do, who you love, and who loves you, your life will improve tenfold. In fact, I strongly believe that when you infuse your thoughts with feelings you begin to manifest. Simply forcing yourself to have good thoughts, or to mantra yourself silly with affirmations, will not help you change your life. You must feel as though what you are aiming to manifest has already happened. Having mastery over your feelings means having a second chakra in balance.

The second chakra is where communion with the *other* is born. It is the center of all relationships from intimate and sexual to those related to work, career, and money. What does that mean? Our womb yearns to be filled in order to create and procreate. In fact, our second chakra is a beacon, or magnet, that can attract anything. We cannot manifest in a vacuum. We cannot create a baby without both egg and sperm. We cannot create art without a relationship to other people, whether they are other artists, collectors, or those who inspire us in some meaningful way.

Relationships are at the center of our lives, as human beings we need others in order to thrive, yet relationships are often the very thing that prevents us from living a peaceful and harmonious life. What creates drama in our relationships is often not the person or situation but how we feel and interpret them or it. We get stuck into what we wish it were, versus accepting people, places and things as they actually are.

Imagine looking at all your relationships, past and present, with compassion and gratitude, no matter what. In fact, let's take an even higher step and assume that all the relationships in our life come and go for a good Divine reason, no matter the hurt or joy we experience from them. By regarding everyone as a teacher, especially those who have hurt us, we can recognize that the lessons people bring into our lives are lessons we've chosen to learn before we came into this world. Let me give you an example: How many times have we heard from a famous actor or athlete that at one point in their lives they were told they would never amount to anything? Is it possible that those naysayers were somehow divinely inspired to say those very hurtful things in order for that actor or athlete to work harder to prove them wrong? In fact, what if there had always been a Divine pact between these two souls, even before they came to life?

Indulge me in a little fantasy and suspend judgment for a minute. Imagine Michael Jordan as a spirit before incarnation, hanging out with another spirit in the ethereal world before coming through his mother's womb and into this world. His conversation about his intentions for his next life could have gone something like this: *"I want to really make a difference in the world. I want to inspire thousands of people, to teach and show them they can achieve the seemingly impossible if they only trust in themselves and are disciplined about their practice."*

The soul buddy replied; *"Okay, I tell you what: I will be your first coach and I will motivate you by telling you that you will never amount to anything. You will hate me and resent me for it, but you will work really hard to prove me wrong."*

Now, see them smile at one another and shake hands. The time comes when they are preparing to reincarnate and they dip into the river Lethe that, as Virgil writes in the *Aeneid*, will erase all their memories and free them to be reincarnated. The two come into this world, one with high hopes and an immense athletic design, the other with such love for his soul buddy that he is willing to sacrifice his life and be hated by thousands. One has come to achieve a great goal, and the other to assist him by being the uninspiring coach taken as the example of a failed teacher.

Can you see the coach as truly loving his soul buddy Michael Jordan? Do you see the sacrifice the coach offered for an entire lifetime? Wouldn't you feel tremendous compassion for him and even admiration after knowing his true mission in life was such a sacrifice?

Whether this really happened is not important. What I am proposing is a shift in perspective. If you look at everyone that comes into your life as someone you have attracted through your second chakra to help you learn a particular lesson, to help you become that which you are meant to be, it could solve many psychological and even physical problems. We know for a fact that resentment and rancor are feelings that create stress, which in turn creates diseases of the mind and body. Using this new perspective as a tool can help you let go of all resentments, develop more compassion for others, and unchain you forever. However, in order to let go you must first know where your feelings come from.

If It's Hysterical It's Historical

I first heard this expression in a 12 steps room. It means that a particularly strong reaction to an innocuous event stems from the activation of a historical memory. Something was said or done in the present that reminds us of a past event perpetrated usually by a primary care taker or peer. The reaction we are having has nothing to do with the present situation but is rather an activation of a historical feeling triggered by what was said or done. Our past leaves trigger buttons that activate old patterns and hurt. *You are pushing my buttons.* We often use this term to refer to these trigger points that makes us do and say things we later regret.

It is as if you are living your life wearing a costume filled with buttons. Each one connected to a complicated wiring system. All the buttons represent something you are hanging onto from an event (historical or recent) that made you feel bad, belittled, abandoned, rejected, etc. Now, imagine that each time someone says something to you one or more of the buttons in your costume are somehow engaged, the electricity runs wild, and more buttons flare up. Sirens go off and your reaction to what is happening has nothing to do with reality. Rather, your reaction is a response to the short-circuiting of these buttons that transform your entire system into an alarmed state. What kind of a life could you have if you removed all of the buttons?

Imagine the kind of encounters you could have if no one could push your buttons to elicit a reaction disproportionate to reality?

When confronted by the conflicts that arise in our relationships we always have a choice in how we react. Instead of living our lives as a series of reactions to these metaphorical buttons being pushed, we can learn from them and use them to better ourselves. Consider the possibility of looking at conflict as an exhilarating challenge, another opportunity to practice and learn. For example, the need to be right and understood is another vestige of the past. Insecurity and fear of not been good enough or accepted for who you are, makes you need to be right and to have everyone to agree with you. This tendency indicates that it is time to delve deeper into self-understanding. What good is it to be right if it prevents you from seeing another person's point of view? After all, how can you ask other people to understand you if you do not understand yourself?

To live a serene and emotionally balanced life means accepting our feelings, disconnecting the emotional wiring attached to our buttons, and choosing our reactions in a way that helps us grow. By letting go of the past and practicing living in the present moment we can learn to live a non-reactive, proactive life.

The following exercise is designed to help you understand your system of buttons and the reactions that ensue because of them. Try it every time you have strong emotions and when you find yourself saying, "*I can't believe I said that, I don't know why I did that.*" Once you learn this exercise it will become second nature to convert instant reaction into a process and an exciting journey of self-discovery. This alone will change your state and therefore your reactions.

Feeling Inventory Exercise

Think of the last time you had a really big fight with someone. Recall the feelings you had during the argument, if you can. What actually happened is not as important as the feelings you experienced in your body. Ironically, often we can recall that we had a big fight, but not the reason why it started, or what brought us to such an explosion. Take your event and run it through these questions and exercises:

1. What am I feeling right now? Or, what was I feeling at the time of the argument?
2. When was the very first time I felt this feeling? Go back as far as you can remember and describe in detail what happened and how old you were.
3. How do I feel as a result of what happened?
4. What did I come to believe about myself as a result of this event and these feelings?
5. Now, look at the present. How do these old beliefs color my life today?
6. Finally, consider this: How would a loving person describe me? How would my Higher Power want to hear me portray myself?
7. Write down a powerful message to yourself that turns these beliefs around.
8. Finally, anchor a physical gesture to the new feelings that arise from this positive affirmation.

Now take a deep breath. Visualize removing the wiring to the button related to this story until it becomes void of energy, essentially turned off. Create an action that will get you out of the funk and anchor it with an empowering feeling. Anchoring is a process of associating a physical action with a new desired feeling. By later repeating this physical action as you recant the affirmation you begin to reprogram your negative reactions giving life to the new positive ones. Don't expect this to work overnight, keep on removing the energy of the past from your reactions of the present, and eventually you will become a pro at this, it will be second nature, like the Aikido master who takes her opponent's energy and uses it to her advantage.

My children and I came up with this little silly dance. If we feel blue, angry, or let down one of us will stand up, bend our elbows and shuffle our arms really fast back and forth together, shaking our hips as we repeat this litany, *"I feel good, I feel great! I feel good I feel great!"* This one inside joke helps us break the negative energy, gets us unstuck and makes us automatically smile, shifting our state and giving us the opportunity to realize where we are.

Feelings Shared - Feelings Heard

After doing this work, many of my clients love to share all their emotions with their partners, but get frustrated if they don't get the reaction they want. A partner cannot always fulfill every need, and expecting them to do so is asking the impossible. Expectations are a set-up for resentments. If we have no expectations we can receive all the gifts that come to us with wonder, excitement and surprise. Before sharing it is useful to ask yourself: *Can I trust this person to listen to what I say without giving me unsolicited advice? Can I trust this person not to take what I say personally and get hurt by my words or feel like they need to fix something? Can I share without expectation?*

When you are feeling the need to share search for a trusted friend, counselor, or spiritual guide. Join one of our workshops and make long-lasting friends on the path to healing the womb.

Remember, you can also share using pen and paper, which is a great tool to both purge and commit your ideas and revelations into this world.

In order to attract a good listener you must first be one yourself. One of the most powerful messages ever given by Jesus simply states, *"Do unto others as you wish others to do unto you."* If you don't like criticism don't give it. If you don't like to be judged or condemned, don't do it. Criticism is futile because it only makes the other strive to justify him/herself and does not bring progress. The same thing goes for complaints. Confucius says, *"Don't complain about the snow in your neighbor's roof when you own doorstep is unclean."* Anyone can criticize, condemn, or complain, but it takes self-control and great character to listen without judgment.

I love the fact that women invest a great deal of energy talking about their feelings, and exploring and understating them. However, beware not to get stuck in the second chakra by reminiscing about the past, or by sharing and rehashing it repeatedly instead of learning from it. As you begin to understand and work on your first and second chakras and respectively your right to be here and your right to express your feelings, you will begin understanding how your emotions play a big part in your well being.

Second Chakra Self-hypnosis

Before you place your womb chakra seed on your altar, nurture it with the following self-hypnosis.

> Lie down and find your own second chakra. Gently place your hands on it and listen with your heart. Your attention will find and settle into that space. Now visualize

your womb and imagine it as a lovely tree with arms outstretched, ready for embrace. Do this even if you no longer have a uterus. Allow the attention to rest where it naturally falls and gradually feel the central stream of energy running up and down through all of the chakras.

Your arteries and your veins come together and embrace one another both at the third chakra and again at the second chakra surrounding your womb. Now ask some questions directly to your womb so you can find out if there's something your womb wants to tell you. Ask: *Is there something I can do to make you feel better? Is there an action I can take, either daily or weekly, to make you feel heard and loved?* Listen and take your time. Some wombs are shy at times and don't immediately respond. Others are chatterboxes. Take time to discern whether or not what you are hearing is mental chatter. Just listen, don't respond. Once the chatter or the silence has gone on for a while, simply make a commitment that you will be back to connect soon. Use this as a daily routine before you get out of bed or just before you go to sleep.

Allow the sound *Vam* to arise and repeat itself at its own speed, naturally coming and going. Hold your attention in the space with both your hands right above the pubic bone. Allow the awareness of water to arise – see the blood flowing, feel its energy flow, and imagine yourself sitting in the middle of its scarlet stream. In Native American legends this is called the seat of the jaguar. It is the seat of creation and the place where you will be able to place all your new ideas, endeavors and dreams. See them grow fueled by trust, not only in yourself, but also in the universe. And, just like that you will witness the Mother in her good pleasure giving you all that you want and desire.

Expect to get amazing insights during these meditations and together with these insights an immediate desire to share them with your loved ones. Write them down!

Closing prayer

I trust my womb and myself. I am willing to feel and express my truth. I am moving toward a time when I am totally happy and fulfilled. Life offers me everything I need for this journey. I am prepared to honor my body and feel good about my sexuality.

The Right to Take Action

Womb Conversation

I honor you, see you and recognize your strength, power, and ability to take the right actions. I accept and value myself exactly as I am.

What risks can I take to strengthen my personal power?

Third Chakra – Personal Power

Third Chakra - The Right to Act

Located in the area of the solar plexus, navel, and the digestive system, the fiery third chakra is called Manipura, the "lustrous gem." This is the center of your gut feelings and self-esteem. This chakra is associated with personal power and the right to take action. Mindfulness in action is closely related to having a clear third chakra. It is in this place that you choose to either thrust forward, confident in your communion with the Divine, or where a void is left that may be filled with food or addictive behaviors and /or relationships. If this energy center is open and flowing it leads to feeling more confident and self-assured so you can use your powers in a supportive, balanced manner. On the other hand, if we have limiting beliefs about ourselves, we may hide our gifts and talents. It is through our actions that we show our commitment to ourselves, to spirit and to the world, not our words. Therefore, not taking responsibility for our actions will keep us stuck in a state of unhappiness, aware of our own lack of honor and not knowing the meaning of our existence. Not surprisingly, most depression comes from a weakened third chakra.

Spins Fast: In Excess, Congestion, Disharmony

From a behavioral point of view, a fast-spinning third chakra creates aggressive tendencies. These tendencies often manifest in the projection of superiority, and in overpowering and forceful behaviors, such as being intrusive, quarrelsome, threatening, pushy, greedy, and intense. From a physical point of view, a fast-spinning third chakra can mean problems with digestion, stomach ulcers, and acid reflux. One who leads with their third charka is someone who is consistently active but experiences burn out, has problems with exhaustion, and often has challenges with food, either through overeating or anorexia. They are goal-oriented, power-loving, ambitious, rebellious, viciously competitive, ruthless go-getters. Emotionally, such persons are often angry and fear intimacy.

Spins Slow: Deficiency, Depletion, Disharmony

The opposite slow-spinning third chakra produces a personality with weak intentions, fragile determination, negative internal dialogues, lack of confidence, an inferiority complex, loss of self worth, and shrinking courage. Emotionally, they experience an inner void, exhibit child-like behaviors, have a weak inner strength, a negative self-image, are disconnected from intuition, and often very lonely. Physical characteristics of a slow-spinning third chakra are manifested in slow digestion, a tendency toward food allergies, hepatitis, liver disease, chronic tiredness, spastic colon, and abdominal cramps.

Balanced – Spins Harmoniously

A balanced third chakra is characterized by a tremendous personal power and yields respect of self and others. Such persons are often spontaneous and uninhibited. A strong leading third chakra gives life to an artist, an intuitive healer, a trendsetter, and a leader, someone with an ability to manifest ideas and to achieve important goals.

Once again, to properly harness and put to use the shadow energies of this chakra it is necessary to remove the rebellious energy of a fast-spinning third chakra. If this rebelliousness can be strategically contained and deployed there is a real potential for true leadership. Conversely, in the slow-spinning phase the tendency toward immature behavior can be transformed into the ability to see the world with child-like wonder.

Honor

The third chakra relates to our right to act. It directly affects our ability to project our will into manifestation. In order to take action we first get to honor ourselves and listen to our intuition. What does it mean to honor the self? Let us ponder this question in the following way:

The definition of honor is fairness, or integrity, in one's beliefs and actions. It is a quality of worthiness and respectability that affects both the social standing and the evaluation of an individual. Many of us are taught about family honor, tribal or religious honor; but very few are shown ways to honor the self.

Imagine this scenario: you wake up from a dream and have the revelation that from now on you should take up a certain activity and change your life radically. Even though you don't really know where this inspiration is coming from, you can feel that it is the right thing to do at a gut level. To your logical mind this idea may sound crazy, yet your instinct tells you to pursue it. Imagine yourself in this confusion, questioning what you know to be true, and then calling someone in order to seek approval. What if your so-called friend, upon hearing of your fantastic ideas, says something like, *"That is a crazy idea. You could never pull it off."* Slowly your shoulders slump, your eyes hit the floor, your breath is shallow and you agree, thinking: "What a crazy idea! My friend is right. I could never pull that off."

What just happened? You disregarded the authority of your own intuition, and your connection to Divine inspiration, in order to maintain the status quo of reason and confusion. You now have dishonored yourself and your path by relinquishing your will to the perception of others. Honoring yourself means committing to your path no matter what others think. If you call upon the universe with the intent to receive a message, and you don't heed what comes, you are in essence telling the universe you do not trust the Divine message filtered through your third chakra.

Honoring yourself also means taking time at night before you go to sleep to run down all the things you are grateful for. It's wonderful to go to sleep appreciating the good in your day and in your life. Honoring yourself is a practice of living with integrity, not lying to yourself or others. You're conscious of your health and take care of your body. Above all, you forgive yourself and are committed to learning and improving your life with love and compassion.

Respect Who You Are

Deep inside your soul you know who you really are, but you're often so busy with life that you suppress the nagging voice that keeps telling you to commit to your authentic self. If you consistently attempt to suppress your authentic self by not putting into action the message received by your intuition, you will eventually run out of energy. Extreme measures get your attention, measures that could literally hurt you. Many people have to have near death experiences before finally embracing the work they were born to do. In healing the part of your energetic field associated with personal power the question becomes: Are you ready to listen to the voice of your authentic self before catastrophe arrives?

We are born into this life with our vocation and purpose intact. At times this purpose reveals itself through a physical sensation – you hear a whisper in your head to do something, or you feel chills running down your spine when witnessing, or even thinking about, a certain thing. A light bulb is turned on in your mind when an idea comes that is in line with your original vocation. These voices and sensations have been there since you were a child. Clues about your calling may be revealed in your mannerism, your personality, or your choices in life. They are the kind of activities you lose yourself in when time passes quickly and effortlessly. Often, your life's purpose is a distant hobby you hardly have time for or pay attention to.

For centuries mankind has asked the questions: *Why am I here? What is my purpose?* Womankind asks questions related to their womb-carrying, baby creating, and nurturing abilities, such has: *What am I teaching my child and how can I help him/ her grow and be a self-respecting individual?*

Regardless of the speed with which the answers come, if we keep asking, eventually our true purpose, including what we'd like to teach our children, will be revealed. However, we find that while we are waiting for things to be revealed, life continues whether we have the answers or not. In my personal journey I was temporarily diverted down an unusual path when I had to get a job quickly to feed my children. Yet, even as I headed down a seemingly contradictory path my persistence in asking the universe to reveal to me my true purpose eventually brought me to the manifestation of the life I was meant to lead.

You have picked up this book, which means that no matter where you are in your life you have begun the process of healing your womb to manifest a new expression of yourself. This is a perfect moment to reflect on where you are or to begin the new journey. Here are some questions that can start the process of understanding and solidifying your life's purpose:

1. What makes you smile?
2. Finish these sentences:
   a. I always wanted to………
   b. I have always been good at……….
3. What activities make you lose track of time?
4. What makes you feel great about yourself?
5. Who inspires you most?
   a. Which qualities inspire you in each of those people?
6. What do people typically ask you for help with?
7. If you had to teach something, what would you teach?
8. What would you regret not fully doing, being, or having in your life?
9. Picture yourself as a 90-year-old woman sitting in a rocking chair. You are blissful and happy, looking back at your life and all that you've achieved and acquired, and all the relationships you've developed. What matters to you most? Make a list.
10. If you had an hour special on television to speak to the largest audience in the world what would your message be about?

Not all of the answers are going to come to your conscious mind at once. However, at the end of this book you will be asked to go through your journal and do something that will help you find the answer to your life's purpose. Make sure you keep a journal and write down the answers to these questions. Record your intuitive thoughts and perceptions. These are seeds you will be placing in your womb to grow and nurture.

An Outsider Looking In

> *"Everyone has his own specific vocation or mission in life... Therein he cannot be replaced, nor can his life be repeated. Thus, everyone's task is as unique as is his specific opportunity to implement it."* Viktor Frankl

We are a unique and wonderful expression of the Universe, God, Mother Nature, or whatever you like to call that which is greater than ourselves. After attending nearly 500 births thus far, I can state with a degree of confidence that each baby is born not a blank slate, they are born with a set of characteristics that are completely unique. We are a combination of nature and nurture. Witnessing all these births has given me a great deal of freedom from the belief that everything I am, and all of my behaviors, come only from my past experiences and my primary caretakers. As a unique individual you have specific gifts you were born with, gifts that once identified can shed further light on your primary vocation.

Look at your life as an outsider looking in – someone with no judgment, someone from another planet with no cultural bias. What are some of the things you would immediately notice about yourself? Do you have a clear picture of who you are as an individual, or are you confused about your identity? Write a few sentences about your uniqueness.

What makes you different?
What distinguishes you from others?

_____

_____

_____

_____

_____

For example, many women have such a natural flare for beauty. It shows in the way they dress, the way they decorate their homes, or prepare a meal. Yet, if you were to call them artists they would deny it, *"Me? No this is just what I do. I am not a true artist."* The artist in you is the ultimate creator having the ability to create babies. Therefore, you can create a new you, a new career, and a new life for yourself. You are the canvas and have access to the raw materials you can use to create the most authentic expression of yourself.

Some women are haunted by the deep-seated belief that acts of self-care equal selfishness. If you are naturally compelled to help others and habitually put yourself last, you may find you are that you ignore even your own hunger or exhaustion. In this case, your life lesson is not about taking more actions, but discerning which actions are necessary. Your challenge is to care enough about yourself to find out who you really are, and to understand the source of this desire to care for others even if it is to your own detriment. Are you giving expecting reciprocity, therefore resenting when you do not receive it? Or, are you one who gives freely for the sheer pleasure of giving? Too often givers live with resentment and exhaustion for they spend their lives waiting for recognition. When our actions are free from expectations, we can exalt our altruistic nature.

What if your best expression is through physical activity? You have always been an athlete, a yoga teacher, a dancer, a tomboy, and a mover. You are grounded in your body and your physical form. You are very tactile, are good at fixing things, and you like to work with your hands. Aging is your typical enemy, menopause a shock to your system. Alas, some women whose true expression is of a physical nature are also those who have terrible relationships with food because they are so entrenched in the way their body is supposed to look. Among these types you find those at the opposite end of the scale. They either work out too much and injure themselves, or constantly think about working-out and dieting to get their body to a certain level. The following questions can help you discover your particular characteristics:

What am I good at?	What do I really want to be good at?
What do I do for others?	What do I do for myself?

Who do I resent for not appreciating all I do for them?	What do I wish to receive from all those I help?
What do I do to get approval from others?	What do I do that makes me feel really good about myself?
How do I feel about my body?	How does my body feel about how you treat it?

To honor yourself is not only to follow your intuition, but also to maintain self-care while doing so. We know that our body has the ability to heal itself and that such healing takes a great deal of energy. As you continue down the path of self-care, ask yourself: What stories am I telling my body? Despite our intention to live healthfully, if we do not have the will to maintain our intent we are actually telling our bodies that healing is not necessary.

Too often we are our harshest judges. We speak to ourselves in a manner we would never allow others to speak to, or about, us. Be gentle and kind to yourself.

I recall watching a documentary on high fashion models, highlighting before and after shots from a previous decade or two. At one point, one of the most beautiful women I have ever seen (a well-known model of the late 40s) was asked about a prized and famous photo of her. The interviewer said, *"People say you don't like this picture, why?"* She responded, *"I hate my feet, you see. My mother told me I had feet as big as a monster and all I can see are those huge feet and nothing else."*

It really does not matter what you look like if you think you are flawed and need fixing. Part of honoring the self is making a commitment to take some time every day to look at yourself in the mirror and express your love and gratitude for the woman who is looking back at you. This can be a very challenging exercise in itself, for many of us are used to looking and seeing only our perceived flaws. However, if you start slowly and commit to smiling at yourself in the mirror and expressing your love for the person you see, it will lead to an amazing healing experience.

When you focus on your third chakra and the importance of your actions you realize that you need to practice mindfulness. Sometimes, in the rush to accomplish necessary tasks, you find yourself losing your connection with the present moment—missing out on what you're doing and how you're feeling. Mindfulness is the practice of purposely focusing your attention on the present moment—and accepting it without judgment.

Mindfulness in Action

Do you remember learning how to drive? At first, every single action was mindful. You got in the car, started the engine, checked the rear view mirror, the seat belt, put the car in gear, carefully looked in all directions, and began to drive to your destination. You were aware and careful of everyone on the road and of your responses. Now, after years of driving, you simply go on automatic and find yourself arriving at your destination without knowing how you got there. Your body took you where you needed to go and your mind went on a journey somewhere else. This habit of mindless driving can show us how we have a tendency to allow our chattering mind to take us away from the now. However, the now is all that exists and staying present is an exhilarating experience.

Try this: become mindful of your daily routines, starting with your morning ritual. Sometimes it helps to describe what you do as you do it. Most of us wake up and go through a ritual of taking care of our body without ever taking care of our spirit. Start with a small change in your daily routine. It takes only five precious minutes to set your intentions for the day and connect your mind and soul to your Higher Self. Practice closing your eyes before you get up and think of three things you are grateful for, and one thing you want to accomplish today. If you think five minutes is too much, just practice one deep breath. Try closing your eyes for one breath and envision going to your third chakra and bringing your attention to your center, your solar plexus.

Everyone has time for one single breath, yet there may be mornings when you forget. When that happens, forgive yourself and move forward, one breath at the time. Eventually, you will find pleasure in sitting up in your bed in the morning and practicing breathing for five minutes until you reach your personal goal of a morning ritual for your body, mind and soul. There is an entire philosophy in Japan called *Kaizen Way*. Rooted in the two thousand-year-old wisdom of the Tao Te Ching, the *Kaizen Way* reminds us, "*The journey of a thousand miles begins with a single step.*" Kaizen is the art of making great and lasting changes through small, steady increments. The idea is that looking at the overall change you want to make in your life can actually work against you. The bigger the change, the more overwhelming, and the less likely you will take the first step. Instead, those who advocate the *Kaizen Way* suggest taking one small step every day toward your goal and not thinking about the final destination. Rather than focusing on the destination, or end goal, simply staying with the next right action can actually bring greater results.

Responsibility

What does it mean to live responsibly? Responsible means having the ability to respond. However, looking deeper we see it is about having the ability to *choose* how to respond. Responding with right action versus reacting out of emotions is living a conscious life.

In your work with the second chakra, you examined ways in which your reactive triggers are set off in certain situations, based on what you learned as a child. You also learned how these reactions are most often an *ineffective* means of communication, typically leading to more conflict, or to unconscious behavior.

The lessons of the third chakra teach us that our emotions are a great guidance system. If an action does not sit well with you then it is out of alignment with your true self. Right action is about your ability to choose your responses, owning your responsibilities and acting with awareness. You are an expression of your most dominant feelings. When a situation presents itself the wisest thing you can do is to consider it a mirror. It has been presented to you for a reason and a lesson. The beautiful truth I have discovered, and that many teachers speak about, is that if you miss the lesson the first time, it will keep appearing until you learn from it. This way you will never lose your opportunity for growth. From this perspective you can understand the rewards that come from taking a moment to be quiet and choosing the action that is right for yourself and the people around you.

Tonight, before you go to sleep, place your hands on your womb and radiate it with all the good you have done and experienced in your life.

Now, it is time to place your third chakra seed on your altar and nurture it with this prayer.

> **Closing Prayer:**
> I accept and value myself exactly as I am. I embrace responsibility for my actions. I am determined to honor and respect myself. My personal power is becoming stronger every day. I choose how to behave in each and every moment with mindfulness.

FOURTH CHAKRA
The Right to Love and Be Loved

Womb Conversations

I send love to everyone I know. All hearts are open to receive my love. I am grateful for all the love I have and will receive.

How can I help you feel my love?

Fourth Chakra – Heart – Love

Fourth Chakra - The Right to Love and Be Loved

The fourth chakra is known as the Heart Chakra because it is located in the center of the chest. This chakra deals with love, courage, and compassion. When it is open you are able to radiate love for yourself and express it unconditionally, and are not dependent on the love of others. In this center the higher spiritual chakras and the lower physical chakras integrate.

Our history of love started in the womb. As we grew up we learned how to give and receive love, and as a consequence some of us have built walls around our heart. Only through forgiveness and vulnerably can we courageously open our heart and use love as a healing tool, healing not only ourselves but also the world around us.

When a person becomes disconnected from their heart the fourth chakra shuts down. This often results in both low energy and shallow breathing. Throughout the ages we have heard many people expressing love as, "he/she took my breath away," as well as in sorrow "when he/she broke up with me, it broke my heart and I stopped breathing." Love, or the loss of it, can indeed take your breath away.

Spins Fast: In Excess, Congestion, Disharmony

When the heart chakra spins too fast, or is too open (placing love above self-respect), the effects are characterized by distortions of loving relationships, and love becomes conditional or possessive. These distortions may also manifest in manipulative behavior, such as emotional withholding to "punish", or a tendency to be overly dramatic. A fast-spinning fourth chakra can produce co-dependency, jealousy, an unrequited craving for connection, an inability to establish healthy boundaries, or failure to see when a relationship is abusive. Physically, you might have problems with the lungs, such as bronchial pneumonia, tuberculosis, asthma, lung cancer and breast cancer.

Spins Slow: Deficiency, Depletion, Disharmony

A slow-spinning heart chakra acts like a wall preventing love from being allowed in, the effects of which can result in a lack of self-love, feelings of unworthiness, and a gloomy sense of self-pity. Generally rooted in a fear of rejection, when the heart chakra is deficient one is obsessed with ideas about loving too much, or unrealistic expectations like waiting for the knight in shining armor. Depletion in this energy center is characterized by attitudes of self-righteousness, blaming, judgment, and dwelling on the failures of past relationships. All those who are avoidance addicts, who isolate and are love anorexic, dwell here. Emotional states include being unforgiving, stuck in anger about a past betrayal, fear of intimacy, loneliness, depression, and grief. Physical manifestations of a malfunctioning heart chakra include heart conditions such as congestive heart failure, palpitations, high blood pressure, and all heart related challenges.

Balanced – Spins Harmoniously

Compassion and self-acceptance reign in the balanced heart chakras. Harmony in this chakra leads to the discovery of the desire for a spiritual experience in all relationships. A balanced fourth chakra yields an altruistic and empathic nature and generally an excellent immune system. In learning from the shadow aspects of the fast and slow-spinning fourth chakra, loving too much can be retooled as the ability to love deeply and profoundly. From needing and craving connection we can develop a strong sense of empathy as well as the ability to connect to a large number of people. Empathizing with the needs of others can be used to serve greater causes such as charities or the community as a whole. Co-dependency can be turned into interdependence. Even the avoidance addict or the person who isolates can discover the joy of his or her own company.

The Gatekeeper

The fourth chakra represents your right to love and be loved. It is the doorway between the chakras of mind and spirit above, and the chakras of self, body, and the material world below. In this center dwells a gatekeeper, standing guard to the threshold of your heart. This figure could be a loving usher maintaining good boundaries and letting in true love or can be the guard that stands in the way of feeling loving, lovable and loved. It is the one that erects a protecting wall around your heart made up of all the beliefs that have been imprinted in your consciousness from the other eight chakras. These imprints come from all you have learned about love from your family/tribe/culture (first chakra), from the experiences with intimate love (second chakra), and from your feelings about yourself (third chakra). The gatekeeper is also influenced by all the things you have heard about love (fifth chakra), the images you have seen about love (sixth chakra), plus all of your personal experiences with love (seventh chakra). Lastly, it is influenced by your relationship with the Divine (eighth and ninth chakras.)

The History of Love

In utero, the baby's needs are fulfilled instantly and automatically. Without asking, the child is constantly soothed by the rhythmic beat of his mother's heart, fed by the placenta, healed by the mother's immune system, and surrounded by a safe environment. This natural and metaphysical connection generates a primordial feeling. *I am completely loved, I am completely lovable, and I am safe.*

Once the baby is born, parents cannot maintain the original feelings of total safety the child felt while on the womb. Laden by the inevitable circumstances of life – work, money, anxiety, sickness, etc. – parents don't always understand the baby's needs, nor can they anticipate or meet every demand. Every unmet need generates a degree of fear and pain, and the child defaults to immature coping mechanisms: screaming or crying to get attention, withdrawing and becoming aloof, or turning into a people pleaser.

Research scientist Bruce Lipton, Ph.D., explains how a child learns behavioral patterns, *"A child's brain can download experiences at a super high rate of speed. From the moment a child is born through about the first six years of life, she is in a super-learning state. Children learn and assimilate from how we treat them and how we respond to each other."* As the baby learns the meaning of love given and received, they are exposed to ways in which love is commonly used by their parents. Sometimes, to restore harmony, the parents use love as a bargaining chip: *"If you really loved mommy, you would not scream at her."* Love becomes a reward for good behavior: *"What a good job you did…Daddy loves you so much."* It can be withheld in anger: *"I am angry at you, you are a bad girl."* Love gets tinted with guilt: *"You should love Grandma, look at all the presents she got you."* It gets religious undertones: *"God loves those who obey Him."* It is given on a timetable: *"Go on and watch some television, Daddy is busy right now."* Showing love in these ways can lead to children learning that love can be used to manipulate others, and that love can hurt and cannot be trusted.

Nonetheless, the loss of love is immediately forgotten each time the child is enveloped in the loving embrace of their mother or father. The sweet feeling of Divine love fills her, and she recalls its primordial origin, how she felt in the womb, and how all her needs were met instantly. But alas, another confusing exchange and love is once more questioned. The gatekeeper continues getting stronger, building walls of protection around her heart.

As we grow and let go of the familial embrace, we discover a new world—the world of our peers. When we start school and are surrounded by an unfamiliar group of people, we discover that their approval, or love, becomes instrumental to our happiness. In an effort to fit in and be accepted by the group, under peer pressure we learn to love only those who are considered acceptable, right, and hip by our group. Concerned only with acceptance and validation, we fall for the cool guy in our school, only to find out (through dating or rejection) that we are completely incompatible. However, because our focus is still acceptance, we don't change our ways. We are on the quest for someone who will reconnect us to the miraculous and unconditional love we experienced in the womb, and we continue our search outside ourselves. We need direction.

Unfortunately, we have no guides in this quest as no one is teaching children about love or relationships. It is not part of the curriculum.

Straying away from our immediate world, we look further for clues about love in fairytales, myths, and the media. Here we are introduced to the impossible and rebellious love of Lancelot and Guinevere, Romeo and Juliet, and Leo and Kate (lovers on the Titanic). We listen to love through the words of love songs and learn that often love equals pain. All these tragedies suggest that true love means losing oneself for the sake of the other. So, we dream of the knight in shining armor to come and rescue us from the tower of loneliness. We look for a romantic, sensitive guy with perfect abs, an amazing smile and wit, just like the hero in the latest movie. We are on an impossible journey in hope, of finding *the one*. At this point, we have actually given a detailed description of the phantom person our gatekeeper can allow into our hearts. Yet, none appears to look like the 'most wanted' poster we provided our heart's usher.

As we mature, we hear mentions that we must love ourselves first, before we can love another. But, no one bothers to give us the tools to do so. The fleeting memory of the original state of wholeness we felt in the womb lingers in our unconscious. We yearn for that heavenly love that can heal us, makes us feel safe, feeds us without being asked, and lulls us without being told. We continue to look outside ourselves for the solution. When we finally find whoever we think is *the one*, we experience sheer paradise. We notice every little thing they do, all the minuscule idiosyncrasies of their character, and we love each and every one of them. We stay up at night thinking about them, we talk for hours, opening our hearts like never before. We become sexier, happier, and more blissful than we have ever been.

Sadly, as time passes, we begin to notice things we had not noticed before. The shadow guarding our hearts is screaming at us, this person does not fit the requirements. It turns out our partners have qualities we can't stand. We expect them to have psychic powers and know what we need or want, and to our surprise, they don't. We demand they satisfy all of our needs, even if *we* don't know what they are. This is not the unconditional love we have longed for. Where is the flawless human being that understands us, makes us feel safe, and offers the type of love *we* are unable to give or receive?

When it comes to love, we have become completely dependent on others, yet based on experiences, we no longer trust anyone to deliver the love we want. Once again, as we did when we were little, we default into immature coping mechanisms and we learn to operate in a codependent manner. Bargaining ensues: "*I will behave this way, if you behave that way,*" or, "*I will show you my love if you show me yours.*"

We manipulate others by placing blame, finding fault, or attempting to control the situation: "*I know you love me, but I wish you told me more often, or in a more romantic way.*" This translates as: "*I am not sure you love me, because you aren't saying the right words, or taking the right actions. Therefore, I can't hear you.*"

We attempt to buy our partner's love by showering them with gifts and favors, disguising our manipulation as generosity and altruism. Some of us enmesh and lose ourselves in the relationship. We compromise our values and integrity; or we minimize, alter, and deny our feelings. There are those of us who need to control and offer advice without being asked only to become resentful when others refuse our help. Finally, we find gratification when someone cannot live or function without us. It appears that our self-worth has been validated and everything seems under control, but we are still unhappy. With one foot in the past we dwell upon what we wish the relationship was, and one in the future where we think about what it could be, we forget about what is and stand on precarious grounds—we are insecure. When all efforts fail to produce the desired unconditional and celestial sense of love we have dreamed about, we resign ourselves to believe unconditional love is a myth. We suppress our dream of the idyllic love and learn to cope with the occasional fighting and the feelings of loneliness we experience in our marriages or committed relationships. We will never be satisfied because we fail to appreciate what *is*.

Byron Katie, who wrote an amazing book called Loving What Is, inspires us with these words of wisdom: "The only time we suffer is when we believe a thought that argues with what is. When the mind is perfectly clear, what is, is what we want."

The Key to Opening Our Hearts

When you are about to go on a new journey, be it a new career, learning a new sport, craft, or art form you give yourself plenty of time to learn. You take courses, you practice, and as you get better you feel more confident, which results in greater success. Yet, it rarely occurs to us that entering a new relationship, one that might last a lifetime, requires spending as much time learning about love as it did learning how to ride a bike, write an essay, or play an instrument.

Often we hear our girlfriends complain that it is so hard to find a man who will commit to a relationship, but women also have a problem with commitment. In our case it is the commitment to ourselves. Our heart needs commitment from a loved one, but most importantly from our self. How often do we get into a relationship with someone simply because they seem to love us, regardless of how we feel about them? At times we stay with someone because we fear being alone, our procreation clock is ticking, or we feel this is the last train that will stop at our station. We have forgotten our heart. Our strategy for loving is colored with the stories of our past and the hurt we've suffered or brought upon ourselves. We linger on memories and resentments, unable to start anew with each and every relationship. In fact, we have armed the gatekeeper to our heart with all these resentments and memories.

The expression *falling in love* encompasses a truism. If we want to love and be loved we must allow ourselves to fall, which can be viewed as a metaphor for trust, without bounds. When we trust that each relationship brings a new lesson required for our growth, and that we have the tools to recover in case the fall ends up being a hurtful one, we begin to let down our walls. We get to open our hearts and forgive ourselves and those who have hurt us. In fact, the key to opening our heart is forgiveness.

Forgiveness creates the space for love to rush in. For this purpose we can transform the gatekeeper of our heart into a celestial bodyguard, free of all preconceived notions, becoming our heart's greatest ally. Actual forgiveness does not mean allowing someone who wronged you to forego his or her karmic debt, nor does it mean condoning or forgetting what was done. Forgiveness recognizes that the road to happiness lies in letting go of the hold that memory has on our reactions, our life, and our perception of self. Forgiving frees us from the perpetrator forever, and those memories no longer have a negative influence on future relationships. In reading *A Course in Miracles*, I learned that my righteous indignation toward what happened in the past conveniently made it seem that others were different from me, that I was good and they were evil. Other people's interests appeared to be separate from and in competition with my own. In that paradigm, others seemed to be forever seeking happiness at my expense. However, when I looked at the perpetrators with forgiving eyes, I saw that their pain and unhappiness was as big, if not bigger than my own.

Forgiveness shows us that we are all the same. We all have the same needs, the same desires, and the same pain. Forgiveness is a gift we give to ourselves, not to anyone else; it is something we can do even before we meet someone, so that we may start anew without bringing the past into our present.

Forgiveness is not about forgetting, it is about letting go. Resentment literally translates as experiencing a negative emotion repeatedly. Resentment is what takes away our serenity in the present moment while not changing the past. Once we can forgive those who have wronged us and let go of resentments, the keeper of the gate will lower our walls and let the love and beauty in. Forgiving and letting go means we must become vulnerable.

Vulnerability

> "The strongest love is the love that can demonstrate its fragility."
>
> Paulo Coelho, *Eleven Minutes*

Culturally, the word vulnerable has been connected with the concept of weakness. Being vulnerable is usually associated with opening yourself up to being hurt emotionally and/or physically. We avoid vulnerability to avoid rejection, but all the while we feel highly uncomfortable by trying to be someone we are not. When we hide who we really are, what we think, and how we feel we are in essence rejecting ourselves. Emotional vulnerability actually requires great courage and strength.

Chris Rock, in one of his stand up routines, says, "*When you meet someone for the first time you are not really meeting them, you are meeting their representative.*" Sometimes, we end up falling in love with this representative only to discover that the person we chose to love is someone different. We also send our representative out on a date in fear that if the person we just met finds out who we really are they surely would not be interested in us.

When we expose our core-self we take a leap of faith trusting that we are good enough and lovable – as is. Vulnerability is the doorway to love and self-love, and gives us access to our inner strength. Dr Brené Brown, a professor and vulnerability researcher at the University of Houston says, *"We emotionally 'armor up' each morning when we face the day to avoid feeling shame, anxiety, uncertainty, and fear. The particular armor changes from person to person, but it usually revolves around one of three methods: striving for perfection, numbing out, or disrupting joyful moments by 'dress rehearsing tragedy' and imagining all the ways that things could go wrong."*

Vulnerability is the experience and emotion we actually crave. We feel most loved when we are accepted for who we are and that can only happen if we show our vulnerable side. Self-protective armor, usually unconsciously erected at a young age, causes most of our adult suffering. Awareness of it is a big step toward freedom. Typically, when we are faced with something that is new and challenging, or that feels threatening to us, we unconsciously retreat behind a force field of self-protection, hiding behind the tall walls we have erected around our heart. Yet, it is the self-protection that creates far more suffering than that which we fear.

Uncertainty and vulnerability are two characteristics we have fought hard to reject in the modern world. In the last two hundred years more women have entered the work force and had to take on the warrior archetype. As warriors we constantly battle and compete. In the business world, expressing one's emotion is considered unprofessional and it is looked down upon as a sign of weakness. As a result, women have had to learn a new game – the game of hiding their feelings. Instead of relying on their instinct toward expansion and expression women have learned to withdraw and choose silence, or opt for aggression and defiance. In this model we come to believe that it is safer to build a wall preventing others from coming close and hurting us, or even worse, from dismissing us as weak and unpredictable.

In the game of the male-dominated workforce, women must look detached, in control, rational and poised. Vulnerability is a sin and women have come to assume a role that goes against their very nature. The constant battle against one's nature and the countless diseases that follow have been the price women continue to pay in order to be perceived as powerful, independent, self-reliant, and successful.

Here is a typical modern scenario.

> Jenny, unable to leave her masculine stance at work, brings her survival mechanisms home. Since multitasking is intrinsic in women's nature she believes she is the only one who can get things done efficiently. Jenny thinks her man cannot handle taking care of a job, marriage, the house, and kids all at the same time. So, she takes on the role of superwoman juggling it all. As a result, she becomes bitter, angry, and condescending with her husband who she sees as an *inferior person*. Someone who wants it all, yet is incapable of managing any part of it, even if she was kind enough to let him. Jenny keeps volunteering to do all of the work herself. She can be controlling even when she seems to only be concerned with pleasing her family. She fears that if she lets them see her vulnerable side, they won't

like, or love, her. She lives on the offensive—attacking, blaming, or correcting others. This keeps the spotlight on others and off of her, once again putting up the armor that keeps people, and love, away.

To reclaim the fourth chakra and embrace love for the self and the world at large we get to let go of the warrior archetype and embrace the mother-nurturer archetype, surrendering to vulnerability along the way. Tuning into our feelings and learning to express them enables us to have a healthy perspective of our problems, our place, and ourselves. After a crisis, notice when the old armor starts to take over. Try to see what thoughts circulate in your mind just before you begin retreating into to your armored self. You will find that fear of what others might think, or of being exposed as not good enough, and ultimately being rejected is responsible for your retreat. You may feel anger, resentment, sadness, fear, or even terror. Try not to fix the fear.

Sit with those feelings and acknowledge them. If you are in a safe environment express them, then prepare yourself to be informed by them. Go through the feelings inventory exercise of the second chakra. Fall madly in love and be curious about who you are and what you need to feel loved and to love. If you do not retreat from your feelings and stay with the discomfort, keeping your attention on the energy/feeling, it will eventually transform into love. Everything reverts back to love eventually. Love for your family, love for your partner, but most importantly, love for yourself and this incredible world we live in.

Become one with the goddess and the mother/nurturer archetype. A goddess is the embodiment of the Divine in a female body. She acts with integrity while loving and nurturing. She lets go of anger, pain, fear, guilt, and judgment. She has no need to change anybody and she does not blame, for she sees the

Divine in all beings. She has learned to love unconditionally and has no expectations. She encourages others and allows things to be what they are, welcoming other people's efforts, she looks at everyone the way a mother looks at her child. She knows that life is a mystery, which cannot be conquered or understood. She embraces her sense of humor, especially towards herself, and feels compassion for all her little idiosyncrasies and human characteristics. She searches for and embraces her Divinity, knowing that change is inevitable and that the journey is as exhilarating as the end result. Sure this is a tall order, but it is what we strive to become, one day at the time. We strive for practice not perfection.

Mastering this journey will make you a living example. Becoming vulnerable will open you up to the heavens.

Using Love as a Healing Tool

In studying hypnosis, I learned of a particular tribe in Africa that believes one way to cure illness is to concentrate on a part of your body that feels good, and then transfer the feeling to the part which is sick or injured. If you were to twist a wrist, you'd concentrate on the wrist that feels good. You would pay attention to all the little movements, all the sensations of wellness in the healthy wrist, and gently transfer them all to the wrist that was injured. We can apply the same method to our relationships with others and ourselves.

Make a list of all the things you love about your partner, and if you do not presently have one, make the same list of all the partners of the past. YES, all of them. Now write down all the things you love about yourself when you are in love, and happy. All you have to do is transfer this love to whatever area of your relationship you'd like to improve, and then see the law of attraction work for you. Let love mend the disagreements or conflicts you are experiencing. Wake up each morning remembering why you fell in love with this particular person and use that to fuel your state of mind. Use this exercise for every relationship that needs mending, including the one with yourself. This is a great tool to use to attract the love and relationship you have been longing for. We hear over and over again that no one can love you if you don't love yourself, but that is not accurate. All kinds of people can love you even if you don't love yourself. However, you may never feel loved unless you are open to witnessing and receiving love from others.

If there is any ailment in your womb this is a perfect time to use this exercise to bring health and well-being to it. If it seems that there is no part of your body without pain, then use the Uterus Mundi: place your hands on your belly and call the well-being of the young womb that brought you into this world or your grandmother's womb where you resided as an egg in your mother's ovaries while she was growing in grandma's belly. Use the wellness of your daughter's womb, your best friend's womb or any woman you like. Go even further and use Mothers Mary's womb, or her mother Anna's womb. Use Rachel's womb if you are Jewish, or Khadīja (Mohammed's first wife) if you are Muslim, According to Buddhist tradition, Queen Māyā of Sakya (Māyādevī) was the birth mother of Gautama Buddha, Siddhārtha of the Gautama, or even use the womb of Mother Teresa, which birthed so much love for humanity. You can transfer their well being into your belly and feel the potentiality of the Uterus Mundi that brings avatars, saints, and unconditional love into this world. This is your tribe and these are your ancestors. Their love lives inside of you. Their love is one with you.

Now it is time to place your love chakra seed on your altar and nurture it with this prayer.

Closing Prayer

The minute I heard my first love story,
I started looking for you, not knowing
how blind that was.
Lovers don't finally meet somewhere,
they're in each other all along.
From *Essential Rumi*

The Right to Speak and Hear the Truth

Womb Conversation

*What I have to say is worthy of being listened to. I pledge
to be mindful of my thoughts and my words. Before I
speak I consider the following: is it necessary, is it true
and is it loving? I am ready to listen to the truth.*

How can I strengthen my voice?

Fifth Chakra – The Throat Chakra

Fifth Chakra - The Right to Speak and Hear the Truth

The fifth chakra is associated with communication, including speaking the truth, finding creative ways for self-expression, and most importantly, silence and listening. It is located at the base of the throat, thus giving the chakra its homonyms name. Mastering this chakra means becoming conscious of the connection between our heart and mind, showing that honesty between those two elements is key to aligning ourselves with our destiny. Our words are in direct correlation to our actions thus the fifth and the third chakras are especially interconnected. What we say, how we speak to ourselves and to others, will influence every aspect of our lives. The throat chakra is also the center of communication to the universe through our prayers and affirmations, therefore personal integrity is necessary for us to thrive.

Spins Fast: In Excess, Congestion, Disharmony

Emotionally, a fast-spinning fifth chakra yields a lot of mental confusion, which in turn generates physical and psychological fatigue. It's like a chatterbox, never standing still in silence or peace, and is seldom ready to listen. This imbalance also manifests with behavioral patterns such as lying, making up stories to be interesting, filling the empty spaces in conversation, and creating drama if we feel afraid of boredom. The voice in an overactive throat chakra will be shrill and loud. It will often interrupt and try to dominate conversations. The general attitude is judgmental with a distinct lack of empathy, compassion, or even interest in the other person. Persons with excess in this regard are not in touch with their feelings and create the illusion of safety through intellectualization and analysis in order to avoid vulnerability.

Spins Slow: Deficiency, Depletion, Disharmony

Those who fear expression inhabit a slow-spinning fifth chakra. The under-active throat chakra produces a constricted whispering voice, often mumbling and whining, timid, and not able to speak up for themselves. This person will find it difficult to initiate a conversation, as if they don't have the right to ask questions. They often forget to tell you something important, and they cannot find the words to express their emotions. Struggles in career are common due to a fear of speaking and negative internal dialogues. Physically, an unbalanced fifth chakra can result in blockages in all the parts of the neck, especially the throat, mouth, teeth, and gums. This energy center also affects the endocrine glands of the thyroid, parathyroid and the hypothalamus.

Balanced: Spins Harmoniously

When in balance, this chakra allows us to fully listen to others, as well as to the subtle voice of our loving intuition, and the many messages divinely whispered to us. Harmony in this energy center can lead to an appreciation for music, great singers, and composers. Good communication, ease in meditation, and artistic inspiration through the communication of words or music are all results of balance in this center. Above all, honesty reigns in a balanced fifth chakra.

To turn some of the negative qualities around, a fast spinning chatterbox can be transformed into a great orator, the timidity we find in the slow spinning fifth chakra can be transformed into a glorious baby whisperer.

Words Are Your Currency

When I spoke about this chakra in my book *Painless Childbirth*, I spent a lot of time concentrating on the importance of being impeccable with our words: say what you mean and mean what you say. Being honest with yourself and others through your expression is important. It marks the difference between conscious living and unconscious actions. If you consider your words to be your currency, something you regard as a treasure that enhances and enriches your life and the lives of those around you, then you can also consider yourself to be extremely wealthy.

Our mouth is both an entrance and an exit used by this chakra. We use our mouth to speak and breathe. We also eat and drink though our mouths, which can lead to the abuse of drugs, food, or alcohol when this chakra is unbalanced. We use our mouth to express our desires and ask for our needs to be met, as well as express judgment, criticism, condemnations, and complaints. We can choose to be honest and sincere, or gossipy and backstabbing. We can express compassion and empathy, or scorn and insult. The vehicle for all these choices is the same – our mouth – and it is up to us to choose one path over the other. On a very basic level we depend on our breathing to keep us alive. Breathing connects us directly to the breath of life. It is said that God has created men by breathing life into clay. The fifth chakra reminds us of the creative power of breath. Inhaling and exhaling consciously can slow a fast beating heart, can allow us to slow down and think before taking action, and reminds us to stay in the moment in our mediation.

Combining Heart and Mind

The fifth chakra's potential is fully exploited when we learn how to communicate and listen with our heart and conscious mind together. If we only speak from the heart, thinking that is the only way to be true to ourselves, then we often unconsciously react from our emotions and fail to take into consideration what our logic and reason tells us. When we only use our mind, we are more interested in being right, putting us at risk of forfeiting the truth to protect our heart and our feelings. In either state, we are usually so invested in our message that we often don't pause to reflect on what was just said. We don't listen to other's responses because we are so busy strategizing our rebuttal as they speak. However, if we pay attention to the silences within the conversation and embrace those spaces, we can connect more deeply with ourselves and with others. This deeper connection is the basis of an authentically engaged and self-actualized life.

We live in a culture that values sharing every thought and feeling as it occurs. Look at how much is shared on social media platforms like Facebook or Twitter. Notice how some people share their deepest feelings and thoughts on a public wall hidden behind their computers. As a result of such blatant over-sharing, we often don't pause to reflect on what we have just said. We blurt out a thought and make it public. However, when we make a conscious decision to sit with a feeling or a thought, paying attention to the silence and the space between our verbal exchanges, we allow the meaning of these feelings or thoughts to be assimilated into our psyches. When we observe without fixating on our internal processes we discover more of who we are, taking in previously hidden aspects, and reconfiguring ourselves. This observation is what allows us to be more deeply authentic in the present moment. By being more authentic we become more self-actualized and can impact our world in powerful ways.

Authentic living is embracing and expressing our truth and communicating our needs in a loving way. But what is our truth? The commonly agreed upon definition of *truth* is that it is used to define something in accordance with fact or reality. However, the so-called truth can be as diverse as its many observers. In order to inhabit your individual truth before speaking as Buddha says, ask yourself these three questions about what you are about to express: *Is it true? Is it necessary? Is it kind?*

Sharing our opinion is not always right even if it is truthful. At times, things might be true and necessary, so it's best to find kind ways to express them. For example, it might be true that your companion eats too much sugar and it might even be necessary for you to share this 'truth' with him. However, unless you share in a loving way you might have a conflict on your hands. Even if it is true and necessary, it might not be your business to tell him what to eat.

Listening to where words (both internal and external) come from will go a long way in keeping peaceful communication with others. At times our truth is not a Universal truth and our need to share comes from the belief that someone else's acceptance or knowledge of our truth makes it more substantial. By definition, if what you call your truth needs someone's acceptance it must not be a *truth*, for reality does not need agreement by others. In other words, you do not need anyone to confirm that the sun is out in the morning even if you cannot see it because of the clouds, the snow, or the rain. The sun rises regardless of your knowing. This is the actual truth. Your feelings about the sun, the rain, and the clouds are also actual. But ask yourself, "Is it necessary that I share my feelings? Is it loving to do so?" Let's say your partner loves the snow and he is really enjoying it because to him it means a fun day on the slopes. On the other hand, to you the snow is a slushy mess that makes everything more challenging. Is it really necessary for you to state or share how much you hate the snow, knowing how much he likes it? Is it kind? Is it considerate?

Practice silence and active listening to bring a lot more serenity into your relationships. You will have better communication because you are reflecting on your motives, words, and actions. Another aspect of this chakra is the act of listening. Listening is not the same as hearing. Hearing refers to the sounds that you hear, whereas listening requires more energy than that. It requires your full attention.

Listening means paying attention not only to the story, but how it is told, the use of language and voice, and how the other person uses his or her body. It means being aware of both verbal and non-verbal messages. Your ability to listen effectively depends on the degree to which you perceive and understand these messages. Listening becomes key in our consideration of the fifth chakra as it relates to the womb, the cradle and receptacle of life's creative force. Gregg Levoy, in his book *Callings*, says, *"If we don't listen our calling goes unnoticed and our life can become absurd (ab-surdis meaning absolutely deaf)."*

Listen to your calling like your life depends on it. Listen as if there is a thief in your house. When you silence your chattering mind you give space to the voice of intuition and can better hear the messages given by the universe. This listening can only be reached through the power of silence.

The Power of Silence

> *"There is no life of prayer without silence. If we really want to pray, we must first learn to listen, for in the silence of the heart God speaks. If you really want to learn to pray, keep silence."*
> Mother Teresa

In the modern world silence has practically ceased to exist. The human race has stamped its authority over the majority of the planet by covering its surfaces with concrete and destroying its plant and animal life. This shift in the planet stifles the natural sounds of the Earth beneath a cacophony of man-made noise. We live against the background of this cacophony, with the jagged mechanical sounds of urban-industrial society continually assaulting our ears. Nothing has done more to obliterate silence than the sound of machines and engines; the roar of cars, airplanes, and trains, the clanging and thudding of machinery, the noise of building and renovating, the chatter of radios and TVs in other people's cars and houses, and music blaring from every conceivable place. In the modern world it's very difficult to go anywhere where there's no possibility of being disturbed by the sound of a passing cars, plane, or boat. The only chance that city or town dwellers get to experience something akin to the quietness that existed everywhere in the pre-car world is in off the beaten path places such as the deserts of middle Africa. However, even in these places small planes flying overhead, or ocean liners sailing the water, can break the silence. The beauty and natural sounds of Mother Nature are missing most of the time.

Not even in the comfort of our own houses can we experience this quality of silence, as now more than ever it is unusual to go into a house where there isn't at least one bit of technology active at all times. Whether this is a television set chattering away somewhere (even if the residents aren't watching it), a radio, a computer, a video game, a washing machine, the refrigerator buzzing 24/7, or the constant and various dings and ring tones of a modern cell phone, our houses are filled with the same external sound stimulation as the world outside of them. In fact, the only sound that is largely absent from people's homes nowadays is the voice of human interaction.

Even among our friends we have changed the ways in which we relate. Today, it is rare to encounter a person who doesn't give in to a quick glance at the phone at least every hour. If we are alone we plug into the world via our computers, phones, iPads, etc. Silence and solitude are the new boogieman, to be avoided at all cost. If we are sad we reach for the phone and type on our phones, sharing our feelings with the world. The same goes for all our emotions. We think we do this because we are a part of a new modern generation who shares, shares, and shares. But in truth, these activities assist us in avoiding personal encounters and prevent us from listening to others.

Most people are no longer used to silence and have even become afraid of it. Along with inactivity, silence has become something that most people are determined to avoid at all cost. Have you noticed how some people need to jump in the second a conversation leads to silence? These kinds of people find a great discomfort in spaces of silence and generate the need to fill them with noise of some sort. However, noise isn't a problem isolated to the outer world. As with the person uncomfortable with silence, the noise inside our heads can also cause problems.

In the same way that the natural quietness and stillness of the world around us is always covered by man-made noise, the chattering of our ego-selves constantly disturbs the natural quietness of our mind. This chattering fills our mind from the moment we wake up in the morning until we go to sleep at night—an endless stream of daydreams, memories, deliberations, worries, plans, etc. in which we seemingly have no control. This endless stream continues in the form of dreams when we fall asleep. In this way, "inner noise" has as many bad effects as the mechanical noise outside of us. By luring us into mulling over all the tiny inconveniences or uncertainties in our life we lend great importance to minor encounters. We end up spending so much time on the little things that we lose sight of the big picture and the things that might be important to our well being. As a result of an over-active mind, we stop living in the present because we're always planning for and anticipating the future, or remembering the past. This constant inner chattering also means that we can never give our full attention to our surroundings and to the activities of our lives.

In today's hectic pace, and the massive amount of external stimuli, and the barrage of information the mass media sends our way, our minds are restless and active. We juggle dozens of different problems and concerns in our brains on a day-to-day basis. Every new thing we see, or every new piece of information sent our way, is potentially the beginning of a whole new train of thought to occupy our mind. Stopping and listening to others, or even to the silence, is nearly impossible. Yet, when we talk about our right to speak, we cannot forget our right to be silent.

In remembrance for those who have passed on, we are often required to take a few minutes of silence to celebrate their lives. Silence is something that is used to honor and respect others. It is a powerful weapon against verbal abuse and it is where God resides. At times, we may have used silence to hurt others by giving them "the silent treatment." However, that is not true silence; it's a lack of interaction. In fact, our mind was probably

GIUDITTA TORNETTA

only pretending to be still and silent as we were probably busy dwelling on what was happening, not quieting the source of our anguish at all. But, when deep silence is observed, we can reach a higher state of consciousness. The first book of the Torah states, *"In the beginning, the earth was a formless void. Out of this void, this stillness, this silence, everything that is, is contained."*

Silence is within you. It is not just the absence of sound or lack of noise. It is the ground, the basis of your very being. In this silence there is nothing to find out and nothing to prove. Just listen with your whole being to what is here now. In music and the performing arts silence is as important as sound and words. A filmmaker can create an extremely dramatic moment using silence—it's simple and effective. Silence is an amazing and powerful state of being that is with you right now. It is you. The only way to find this inner silence is to stop everything else. Today many centers and workshop leaders offer silent retreats in which participants are obliged to simply be with the self. I highly recommend those retreats, but you can also practice silence by creating time to be silent, perhaps an hour a day or an entire day a month.

Personally, it is one of hardest practices I have ever attempted. I am a chatterbox. I love talking, and as a teacher I do a lot of talking. So, the first time I went into silence I thought I was going insane. I have trouble not talking to the person in line behind me at the grocery store let alone going for several hours without talking to anyone else. At first I had expectations that the stillness and silence would help me figure out all kinds of major questions. However, I quickly realized that at first what silence gave me was a window into my overcrowded mind. The idea behind this practice is to perform a deep cleaning of the deepest recesses of the mind, which initially can bring up a lot of painful memories. Sitting in silence is like shutting the curtains and really studying the walls of your mind. You may find out that there is some serious re-arranging that needs to be done. When strong memories and feeling arise from this practice make sure you enlist some trusted friends and even professionals to help you navigate through what transpires.

During this silent practice, which can equate to a daily meditation, just observe, don't react. A deliberate effort is made to restrain the wandering of the mind, either by slowing down the thought process itself or by developing a means of detaching oneself from it. When emotions are observed, not suppressed or amplified, they filter through quicker, leaving a smaller residue behind. Sensations rise and pass. Look at your emotions, as you would notice a leaf floating down stream in a river. You don't need to pick it up, change its path or re-arrange it. You could choose to just observe the leaf and let it go on its path down the stream.

Listening to the Messages in Your Head: Self-Talk Inventory

Most of us are unaware of the chatter that runs through our minds while we are doing other things. Our thoughts are the construction tools with which we build our reality. To change our thinking, it's necessary to become aware of our thoughts.

A number of years ago the National Science Foundation estimated that our brains produce as many as 12,000 to 50,000 thoughts per day. What's disturbing about these 50,000 thoughts per day is that the vast majority of them are pure nonsense. The same study estimated that upwards of 70-80% of our daily thoughts are negative. We often obsess about mistakes we might have made, battling guilt, planning ahead, or worrying. We are constantly drifting into fantasy, fiction, and negativity. The human mind appears to be wired for neuroticism.

A healthy first step to alleviate this problem is to increase one's awareness of these negative and bogus thoughts. This exercise is designed to assist you in becoming aware of the quality of your thoughts throughout the day. Chose one entire day where you will be the non-judgmental observer of your mind and keep track of your thoughts. Jot them down on a piece of paper that you will carry with you everywhere. Try to suspend judgment. If you find you are beating yourself up about the many negative thoughts you discover, add those thoughts to your list as well. For those of you who already meditate, this process will likely not be surprising because you are familiar with the "monkey mind" phenomenon in which the mind is observed as an out-of-control thought generator. On this day, ask yourself the following:

+ What kind of things do I say to myself? Write down the good, the bad, and the ugly.

   _____

   _____

   _____

   _____

+ Under what circumstances do I most notice my self-talk increasing?

   _____

   _____

   _____

   _____

✦ What are some of the things I say or think about myself?

_____

_____

_____

_____

✦ What are some of the things I tell myself about the actions and activities I do?

_____

_____

_____

_____

✦ What thoughts do I have that are loving and supportive of my desires?

_____

_____

_____

_____

✦ What kinds of thoughts are repetitive? When have I heard those thoughts before, and from whom?

_____

_____

_____

_____

Make a list of your most repetitive thought patterns and the times you have heard them before.

Recurring statements	Who said them	How it made me feel

Unless we become familiar with our habitual thought processes, and commit to making changes, we will remain stuck – in fact, we'll be immobilized by our patterns and habits.

Negative Self-Talk as a Habit

After completing the previous exercise you'll know some of your thought patterns better and your habits of negative self-talk. As we have previously discussed, the majority of our thought patterns are negative, and for most of us this includes negative self-talk. However, you cannot simply let go of the habit of negative self-talk without replacing it with a positive one. Studies have shown that you can only focus on changing one habit at the time. To start the healing process start by changing one recurring self-judgment you catch yourself repeating often.

Let me give you a personal example of a bad habit I had to change. For many years, when I'd stop by a mirror, I would make funny faces at myself, paying attention to what I did not like in my appearance and making harsh judgmental comments to my own reflection. Once I became conscious of that habit, I began switching the remarks with gibberish. I had to take small steps because simply reversing the messages with positive ones seemed disingenuous. What I noticed at first is that I replaced the words with strange and judgmental facial expressions accompanied by silly but aggressive negative gibberish. I then began simply changing the gibberish and the facial expressions adding a smile here and there and a funny face that would make me laugh. It took a long time for me to stop judging myself, but slowly I began looking at my image and saying, *"I love you, you are so cute."*

Today, I wake up in the morning, look at myself in the mirror and say, *"Hi baby, how are you! I love you. Have a good day."* During the day, if I catch myself looking into the mirror to check out my outfit or my hair before I leave, I make sure to add, *"You are beautiful."* The more I say it, the more I feel it and believe it.

Chose one of your habits related to self-talk or thought processes and find a new way of talking to yourself. Changing even just one habit can change the way you live your life and bring you a lot more silence and serenity.

Honesty: Our Bodies and the Universe Are Listening

Our body listens to our words and pays attention to our actions. Our words are an example of our honesty and integrity. For instance, if you ask and pray for your body to heal your aching liver, but you keep on drinking, your body will register that your desire to heal is not reliable; in essence your request has no integrity. Why should your body heal itself if you are not committed to the healing process?

The Universe will grant all your requests as long as you do your part. Do you know what you really want? You might answer, *"Well, of course I know! I want to be happy, healthy, and more prosperous! What a silly question! Everyone wants that!"* Yes, it is true. We all want those things, but how do we ask for them? And more importantly, are our actions consistent with our requests? When it comes to successful relationships, money, and health do you find yourself saying things like: *"I never get what I really want,"* or *"That will never happen to me."* When we pray we often plead to our God the following way: *"Please God, I need money to pay this bill,"* or *"Please God, I don't want to be sick anymore."* What we are really expressing is our fear about lack of money or health. Furthermore, by pleading in this manner we buy into the concept that we are separate from God and that we live a life of limitation. As you recite this type of prayer, you may be wondering where this miracle is going to come from, or if you even deserve what you are asking for. When you say, *"I don't want to be sick anymore,"* you are concentrating on what you don't want, and you will get more wanting to feel better instead of actually feeling better. When you focus on what you don't have, your energy is in the wrong place.

Have you thought about the exact thing that you want? Have you dreamed as big as you can dream? Do you really feel, deep inside, that you deserve it? Do you think your Higher Power loves you enough to happily give it to you?

Our commitment to the message is more important than the message itself. If you ask to feel better, you are not really asking to be healed. If you are asking for some peace, you are not asking for complete peace. Try changing your words and act as if you have already received what you've requested, and don't forget to take the right action to show the universe that you are honest and committed to your desires. State your prayers as if they have already happened: *"Dear God, I am grateful for the health and happiness in my life."* By affirming your gratitude for what you already have the universe responds by giving you even more.

Words and prayers are not enough. You get to combine theory and action in order to receive anything, including love. Eric Fromm, in his book *The Art of Loving*, tells us that even love requires learning and taking actions. Even love is work.

> *"The first step to take is to become aware that love is an art, just as living is an art. If we want to learn how to love we must proceed in the same way we have to proceed if we want to learn any other art, say music, painting, carpentry, or the art of medicine or engineering.*
>
> *The process of learning an art can be divided conveniently into two parts: one, the mastery of the theory; the other, the mastery of the practice."*

Simply desiring to be in a loving relationship, requesting and praying for it as if it has already happened without taking action will not bring results. The strongest most enduring relationships take work. Even a healthy relationship is like a garden; it's a beautiful thing, but you wouldn't expect it to thrive without a whole lot of labor and TLC.

Abundance is no different, just saying that your life is abundant is not enough to create abundance because the universe knows when you are faking it. The universe, your body, and your mind work on faith and action. Through faith and action, Abraham and Sarah had a child at the age of ninety. Through faith and tremendous action, Moses parted the sea. Through faith and action, Jesus raised Lazarus from the dead. They did not linger, they did not plead; they forged forward with faith. Abraham and Sarah created a tribe that today is recognized as the Jewish people. Moses took all the Jewish slaves out of Egypt and led them into the desert to the Promised Land. Jesus spent his time preaching and teaching and sharing his love for God. It is with faith and action that miracles manifest. Check inside yourself and see if you have capacity for faith and action to work hard for the things you have been asking for in your prayers. Know in your heart that you deserve to follow your bliss.

Now, it is time to place your throat chakra seed on your altar and nurture it with this prayer.

> **Closing prayer**
> *My God is the God of plenty and I now receive all that I desire or require, and more. To do this today I will take the following affirming action:"*
> (Then declare your action and act on it!)

The Right to See and Know the Truth

Womb conversation

I recognize your vision and your insight.
I see you, and I appreciate you.

How can I show my love for you?

Sixth Chakra – Sight and Insight

Sixth Chakra - The Right to See and Know the Truth

The sixth chakra is the third eye chakra located between the eyebrows. It is also referred to as the brow chakra. Its Sanskrit name, Ajna, which can be translated as "Command," refers to one's capacity for clairvoyant intuitive wisdom and the ability to see the truth. The sixth chakra is associated with both light and the power of visioning. The power of light is wisdom through contrast and duality; there can be no light without darkness. The power of light opens your imagination and the ability to visualize. This chakra provides a source of inner knowing as well as the capacity to see an objective reflection of how things are. People with clear sixth chakra focus on a commitment to the truth, and have flexibility of thought, giving them a sense of life's realities that surpass usual conscious barriers.

The sixth chakra is the energy center that governs the mind. Its primary polarity for balance and integration is with the 2nd Chakra, the womb. With a crystal clear intention, you can plant your dream-seed (conceived in the sixth chakra) into the fertile soil of your womb (second chakra) and with discipline and hard work (third chakra) you can stand witness to that seed and observe it mature into reality.

To create your reality you must first discover how you mind works, are you primarily a visual person, or do you prefer to use your auditory or kinesthetic abilities to reach your goals? Self knowledge of how we learn is of extreme importance, we cannot use a simple one-fit-all methodology to our manifesting. Your personal vision and manifestation ritual must be in alignment with to how you, and your unconscious psyche, produce its greatest results. This can mean the difference between success and failure. Wisdom from the sixth chakra and compassion from the second come together to strengthen the belief that your desires and dreams are achievable.

Spins fast: In excess, Congestion, Disharmony

Emotionally, a fast-spinning sixth chakra creates overpowering personalities that live in a fantasy world. An excess in this energy center leads to highly logical, dogmatic, authoritarian, and downright arrogant individuals. Migraines are often plaguing those with an imbalance in this chakra. Additionally, characteristic to this type of disharmony are people who have no time to hear others, exhibit a know-it-all personality, and often suffer from hearing difficulties.

Spins Slow: Deficiency, Depletion, Disharmony

People who suffer from a blocked sixth chakra tend to suffer from symptoms like blindness, spinal problems, panic attacks, poor eyesight, seizures, learning disabilities, and a fear of facing truth. They are often undisciplined, fear success, and set their sights too low. They have a tendency to get lost in the details and are unable to finish a project. Dysfunction in the sixth chakra may also be associated with problems of physical growth as our biological structure changes in accordance with our perception of self. Our ability to separate reality from fantasy, or delusion, is in direct connection with the imbalance of this chakra.

Balanced – Spins Harmoniously

A balanced sixth chakra yields a charismatic, highly intuitive individual not attached to material things. This person is someone who may experience unusual phenomena. When the brow chakra is balanced, the individual interprets reality free from his or her own illusions. The perfect example of a dominant sixth chakra would be a player in Herman Hesse's *The Glass Bead Game*. In this book, the players were able to look at the big picture interweaving knowledge and wisdom from as many sources as possible. Another more popular example is the work of Joseph Campbell who spent his life finding common denominators in myths from several difference cultures around the world. He exposed the commonality of our belief systems and helped us realize that we are one and the same with all human kind. To turn around some of the fast and slow spinning characteristics mentioned above, one could see how those who seem to prefer details have the potential to rejoice in the beauty of small things. A know-it-all could become a great investigator of knowledge.

The Right to See

The sixth chakra is closely related to vision and goal making. Visualization and imagery are powerful tools you can use in all stages of life. From launching and growing a business, birthing a baby or a new you, to making a career change, visualization helps you stay on top of your game when making important phone calls, meeting with clients about potential opportunities, and goal setting. Not only does visualization prepare you to take action, it enhances motivation. When you clearly visualize the outcome you want in vivid details and really feel how it feels to succeed, it's hard not to get excited about taking action. Researchers have discovered that the vivid images in visualization exercises can produce subtle but real firings along the neural pathways. These firings essentially prime the body for the physical act itself. Your central nervous system does not differentiate between real and imagined events. In essence, sharp mental images, in which all of the senses are involved, are capable of "priming" and "pre-training" the body for a particular activity – whether it's downhill skiing or giving a client presentation. This creates a pathway or connection between mind and body that promotes smoother and more precise physical activity once you actually take the action you've visualized.

However, the opposite is also true. Instead of seeing things as they are we see the reflection of our own state of mind. For example, two people can enter a room and, depending on their state of mind, have completely different experiences. One, happy about her life and how things are, can walk in and notice beautiful objects around the room and focus on the two people who smile at her. Another, who is burdened by constant judgment, will notice what is misplaced or wrong in the room and the people who seem angry, unhappy or not to be trusted. Our experiences of the world around us largely depend on the dialogue that goes on in our minds and how we process information. To learn how to change or modify the way our inner dialogue works we need to learn what our predominant way of learning is. As I tell all my clients, there is no such thing as one method that works for all. We must know how we assimilate information best and re-learn accordingly. Understanding these subtleties helps me a great deal in my private practice. It enables me to craft the hypnotic script which can best reach my client's unconscious to either help them either heal from a past negative experience or manage the waves of labor.

Visual Auditory Kinesthetic Learning

A common and widely used model of learning is Fleming's (2001) Visual Auditory Kinesthetic (VAK) model. According to this model, most people possess a dominant or preferred learning style. However, some people have a mixed and evenly balanced blend of the three styles:

1. Visual learners
2. Auditory learners
3. Kinesthetic learners

If you are primarily a visual or auditory learner your sixth chakra is highly developed. If you are a kinesthetic learner your second chakra is more dominant. Of course, most of us are a combination of the three. To find out which one you are there are some great tests you can do online by searching the VAK test. When we deal in the sixth chakra on the power of visualization we need to be aware of how we perceive and process the world that surrounds us. For instance, I am a highly visual person and there is no way I can work or even meditate if my environment is not tidy. For me, visual order can dictate not only my state of mind, but also whether I can sit down and write, begin a new project, or even rest peacefully.

In their book *Willpower*, Roy Baumeister and John Tierney explain that the necessity for order might be true for all of us, even if it seems one does not care much about tidiness.

"Another simple old-fashioned way to boost your willpower is to expend a little of it on neatness. … people exert less self-control after seeing a messy desk than after seeing a clean desk, or when using a sloppy rather than a neat and well-organized Web site. You may not care about whether your bed is made and your desk is clean, but these environmental cues subtly influence your brain and your behavior, making it ultimately less of a strain to maintain self-discipline. Order seems to be contagious."

If you want to see how important order is in your thoughts and practice, try using what is called the bright-line rule. The bright-line rule is a clearly-defined rule or standard, generally used in law, composed of objectives that leave little or no room for varying interpretation. For instance, if you tell yourself that you want to increase your physical activities you are creating a fuzzy-line. There is too much room for different interpretations. However, if you imagine and commit to a half hour of yoga, or a walk every day, you have created not only a bright-line but also a simple visual you can see with a specific goal you can accomplish.

Interestingly enough, even auditory learners need order and the auditory counterpart of bright-lines, which is harmony. I recently heard of an amazing story that demonstrates how much our brain and our hearing need order. When *The Rite of Spring* ballet and orchestral concert by the Russian composer Igor Stravinsky was first performed at the Théâtre des Champs-Élysées on May 29 1913, the avant-garde nature of the music and choreography caused a sensation and a near-riot in the audience. At the time, a Parisian ballet audience typically consisted of two diverse groups: the wealthy and fashionable set who would be expecting to see a traditional performance with beautiful harmonic music, and a "Bohemian" group who would be more susceptible to new and avant-garde type of music. The reason behind the near-violent reaction has been attributed to the experiments in tonality, meter, rhythm, stress and the dissonant character of the music. The wealthy and fashionable did not accept the unfamiliar sound and booed the performance, fighting with the bohemians who were intrigued by the very non-traditional nature of it.

Author Daniel Levitin in *This Is Your Brain on Music: The Science of a Human Obsession*, says that the brain tries to predict music before it happens. Going back to the Stravinsky example, until 1913 all music was somewhat melodic and harmonic. When the first non-melodic music was heard in *The Rite of Spring*, the audience's brain was not prepared for it, their ears could not create an order that could be catalogued and accepted by the brain, thus the unrest. The publicity this near-riot created resulted in greater exposure to the music. Eventually, the public grew accustomed to the new sound – the brain found order. When the same ballet was performed again at the same venue in 1920 it was hailed a great success. The ballet is now considered to be one of the most influential musical works of the 20th century.

In a recent radio interview Levtin said, "*We did some experiments in my laboratory that show that listening to music changes your brain chemistry.*" It turns out, listening to enjoyable music, whether familiar or new, makes our brains release dopamine. Levitn continues, "*And we know that people use music the way they use drugs. A lot of people have a certain kind of music they use to get out of bed in the morning to help get them going, to get them started, to help them finish an exercise workout.*"

We know that every type of reward, whether visual, auditory or tactile increases the level of dopamine in the brain. Dopamine, known as the pleasure hormone, is a neurotransmitter that deals with feelings and leaves you blissful. It follows that what we see and hear not only changes our brain chemistry, but leaves us wanting more.

Now, let's look at the kinesthetic aspect of the biology of learning. Aside from dopamine that is released through visual, auditory, kinesthetic "familiar and pleasurable" experiences, there is another hormone our body creates during pleasure (i.e. visualizing your goals viscerally) that comes into play. Endorphins are feel-good chemicals produced by the pituitary gland and the hypothalamus. This chemical is a natural painkiller which lowers stress while inducing a general sense of well being, causing feelings of euphoria and relaxation. Endorphins have also been attributed to increases in confidence. Kinesthetic people learn through physical activities. Laughter, physical contact, exercise, excitement, and even consuming chocolate can increase their endorphin levels. Additionally, dopamine is an addictive hormone and often we seek its release through various activities. On the other hand, low levels of dopamine and serotonin are, in some cases, responsible for depression. If we become aware of what increases the levels of endorphins and dopamine in our system, we can manage depression and mood swings by managing our visual, kinesthetic and auditory perceptions. What we look at and listen to, and who we touch and are touched by, can determine how we live our lives, how we reach our goals, and how we obtain peace of mind.

Your Touchy Feely Harmonious Vision

Visual people, it is time to create a Vision Board, a collage of images and words that represent the things you wish to attract into your life. Traditionally, they are made out of poster board, corkboard or similar material and then filled with pictures, words and phrases, either taken from other sources (magazines, newspapers, etc.), or from self-made elements. The main idea here is that by surrounding yourself with these images that represent your heart's desire and by taking a little time to focus your attention on the images, you are intentionally putting yourself in vibrational harmony with your desire. Thus, opening the door to allowing these things to come into your life more easily and readily.

If you are predominantly auditory, create a series of music lists to listen to while you go about implementing each step you need to reach your goals. Also, one thing that has helped me tremendously is to create a recording of my voice expressing all the gratitude I have for the gifts received. In 2001, I made a recording filled with true felt emotions about what I wanted to achieve. I spoke in the present tense in a key of gratitude reviewing all the gifts at the end of my day. It began with me driving home after a fulfilling day, envisioning my first book published and being surrounded in my doula practice with satisfied and loving clients happy to pay for my services. I expressed the joy and gratitude, and even the surprise at the accomplishments my Joy In Birthing Foundation, the nonprofit arm of my company, had achieved in helping mothers create the birthing experience they desired. I saw myself traveling, teaching, and having good friends all over the world. I was specific to the towns in which I had visited and had friends. At the time I made this recording, I hardly had any clients, had not published my book, and did not have a company let alone a non-profit foundation. Nor, had I ever taught or traveled the world doing so. All this and much more has now come true. Sure there were some details that were not precisely fulfilled, but God's plan has proven far better than anything I could have imagined.

For those of you who are primarily kinesthetic, place yourself physically where you want to be. Close your eyes and feel with every cell in your body what it would feel like to have reached your goals. I had a friend who dreamed of winning an Oscar and she would go and purchase a ticket to a show in the same theater the Oscars are given. She'd go a little early before the performance and squint her eyes so that she could still see the stage and see the people coming in, but the image would be blurred enough that she could add the fantasy of hearing her name called first as a nominee, and then as the winner. She would then rise from her seat and slowly walk down the aisle feeling like a winner. Having memorized her acceptance speech, she would deliver it at the base of the stage in a whisper. Sure she would get strange looks by the people who were trickling in, but she did not see them, she was detached from them, and all she could feel was how her blood was bubbling in her veins dancing with joy for receiving an Oscar for her work as an original screenplay writer. Has she won? Not yet, but she has indeed published her first book and is writing her second.

How We See and How We Are Seen

In a recent Dove commercial, called *Dove Real Beauty Sketches*, an FBI forensic artist sketched a series of women based purely on the way they described themselves and again as others described them. The artist could only hear the voices of their subjects, but could not see their faces. A video about the experiment, which has been viewed on YouTube more than 55 million times and counting, revealed the stark difference between the way the women saw themselves and the way others saw them. Across the board, the self-described portraits were the least attractive – suggesting, according to the Dove marketing team, *that we are all more beautiful than we think we are.*

We live in a difficult world where images of what a woman should look like are decided by the media and fashion magazines. Computer software is constantly used to distort reality before any photos are published. We are a culture that aspires to be what is impossible to be – perfect, unblemished, with faultless symmetry. You'll get a chuckle at knowing that in the past I was a producer and director for the Playboy TV Channel, and in part responsible for perpetrating such fallacy. I recall at times meeting Miss March or Miss September and not even noticing their playmate potentiality until they had gone through a two-hour makeup and hair session.

The constant barrage of "perfect" (unrealistic) images creates a comparative response in all of us. Comparing can be an addictive behavior and leads to sadness, anger, jealousy, and dissatisfaction. In today's social media frenzy of in-your-face tallies, and status updates and photos of happy-looking people having great times, some people can feel inadequate and even depressed if they think they don't measure up. When we compare ourselves to others, we do a disservice to all.

When you look at yourself and others with compassion, love and acceptance you will notice that everything and everyone is special. We all have a very important part in this universe, and we have all been given many lessons to teach and learn. Nothing is superfluous, unimportant, or unnecessary. There are no mistakes for those who care to pay attention. When you find yourself spending time making comparisons, ask yourself the following questions: *What am I to learn from this experience, or from this person? What am I to understand about this feeling I have of being less or more than someone?*

Our eyes are the portals to the world without that scans the universe either for beauty or for what is wrong. We can look and compare or find and discover. The choice is ours.

Your Perception of What Is

Do you feel beautiful?	How do you react when someone offers you a compliment?	What can you do each day to notice the beauty that surrounds you and the beauty that you are?

Now, let's look at the way you see yourself physically. Find a quiet place where you will not be disturbed and do the following. Take your clothes off (yes all of them!). Turn up the light and stand in front of a full-length mirror. As you look in the mirror, write down what you see:

Terrific Parts _____

Good Parts _____

Okay Parts _____

Bad Parts _____

Horrible Parts _____

Now, while you are standing there, write down how you feel about what you are looking at. What kinds of thoughts do you have about your body? Instead of thinking in terms of good or bad, try to identify the feelings like shame, pride, revulsion, happiness, sadness, sexiness, anxiety, disgust, detachment, and embarrassment.

_____

_____

_____

_____

_____

_____

_____

_____

_____

_____

As you look at your naked body, try to picture your ancestors – your mother, her sisters, your grandmothers, and others in your family. Try to identify which parts of your body are directly attributable to genetics:

_____

_____

_____

_____

_____

_____

_____

Go ahead, get dressed and find a quiet and comfortable place to sit down or lie down, close your eyes and meditate on your answers. Do this for at least 10 minutes, and then write down what has transpired.

_____

_____

_____

_____

_____

_____

_____

_____

Picture yourself in an aerobic class or running the marathon or dancing at a nightclub. How does your body feel as it moves through space? Do you feel agile and in control or do you feel clumsy and awkward? Does your body respond to what you tell it to do? Or, does it have a mind of its own? Is it graceful like a swan, or clumsy like an ostrich trying to fly? Try to describe in one or two sentences how your body feels when it's moving:

_____

_____

_____

_____

_____

_____

_____

_____

Before proceeding to the next exercise, close your eyes, lean your head back, and take some deep, relaxing breaths.

Picture yourself as a young girl, perhaps five or six. What kind of messages do you remember hearing about your body?

Were you praised for being a good eater or criticized for being a picky one? Where you taunted with being called a "Fatty or Fatso" or "Skin and bones"? Did anyone comment on your baby fat or beanpole legs? Where you praised for your ability to turn somersaults and hang by your knees or laughed at for bungling hopscotch?

Write down the most memorable messages from your childhood:

_____

_____

_____

_____

_____

_____

_____

After this exercise it is a good idea to find out what core beliefs you learned at this age, and from whom. Imagine that you have looked upon your daughter's body, would you say to her the same things you are telling yourself? Would you use the same words? Now, try to imagine that your daughter has just shared how she feels about her body with you, what would you tell her? How would you help her let go of the negative thoughts? What would you suggest she do to forgive herself, forgive her heritage, embrace her goddess within and let go of any and all worries and preoccupations? Feel the love of your mother-self and then become willing to let go of any negative core belief. Ask God to remove them from you, and forgive those who helped you believe in them or create them. When a woman believes she is authentically beautiful, she frees herself from the overwhelming prison of self-doubt and unworthiness – she instantly becomes a role model for other young boys and girls.

Wisdom and Compassion –
Sixth and Second chakras

> *"Frequently people think compassion and love are merely sentimental. No! They are very demanding. If you are going to be compassionate, be prepared for action".* Archbishop Desmond Tutu

Activating the energy of the third eye leads us to wisdom – becoming the co-creator of our own reality. Through the reasoning mind we can understand what motivates us to do things, but it is the deep awareness of our inner truth that drives us to create what our higher self desires. Our brains run our physical bodies, but our womb/feeling center controls the energy body. In this way our thoughts create energy and our womb/feelings can then bring it into manifestation. Any thought that we have can lead to fruition, be it negative or positive. It is up to the sixth chakra to encourage the mind to only produce conscious thoughts, and it is up to the second chakra to reinforce them with strong feelings. Vision and insight are intertwined with our intentions and emotions; clarity and follow-through are instrumental to reach our goals. The need to create more cohesion between these forces is required.

In one of his lectures the Dali Lama said, *"The Buddha taught that to realize enlightenment, a person must develop two qualities: wisdom and compassion. Wisdom and compassion are sometimes compared to two wings that work together to enable flying, or two eyes that work together to see deeply."*

I see the sixth and the second chakras working in tandem; the mind's wisdom needs the womb's love and compassion to become enlightened, to "see" the light, know the light and be the light.

Closing Prayer

As I let go of all expectations, I trust that my imagination will create a world of happiness and security for me. I detach with love and compassion from the images of what I should be, and embrace what is with all its magic and uniqueness.

The Right to Live a Conscious Life

Womb Conversation

*I release all limited beliefs and lift myself up to higher
levels of awareness. I experience with my sacred
moon blood the birth-death-rebirth cycle*

*How can I hold you as you expire in my arms? How
can I welcome the new you with open arms?*

Seventh Chakra – Consciousness

Seventh Chakra - The Right to Live a Conscious Life

The seventh chakra is located at the top of the head and opens upward. Also called the crown chakra, it is often represented in religious paintings as the halo above the head. It is associated with a profound spiritual connectedness to the infinite intelligence that exists in the universe. This chakra is the seat of higher wisdom and the energy that comes from it. This is also where *the dweller at the threshold* lives. As with the fourth chakra, where we had a shadow-figure standing guard to our heart, the dweller of the seventh stands at the doorway between heaven and earth, at the door through which the Divine becomes incarnate. The dweller represents all your challenges and resistances, the lessons that need to be learned and those things that need to be released before the godhead can come through and infuse all the now opened chakras that reside in your body. However, once you have embraced the lessons the dweller becomes the midwife that helps facilitate and open the door for Divine energy to express Herself through you. Here the old you must die for the new expression of the Divine you to come through.

Spins Fast: In Excess, Congestion, Disharmony

Emotionally, a fast-spinning seventh chakra can result in a sense of being lost or disconnected from reality. One can become a cult leader or a righteous religious organizer, a missionary who believes his way is the only way, his God is the only God. The physical parts of the body that relate to this chakra are the brain and head, the pineal and pituitary glands, and their hormones. Symptoms of imbalance are: an inability to connect to the physical world, confusion, headaches, mental illness, hallucinations, and an overriding ego. People who have no harmony in this chakra want to dominate others but have little or no knowledge of their own powers and tend to be overbearing.

Spins Slow: Deficiency, Depletion, and Disharmony

With a slow-spinning seventh chakra you can experience the sense of being constantly exhausted, foggy and confused, as well as frustrated from an inability to make decisions. It is also when our trust in a benevolent God, or world, can go awry and where paranoia lives. In this paranoia, one might experience feelings of betrayal or disappointment; feeling lied to by God or religion. The result is a lack of inspiration, limiting beliefs, and no spark of joy. People with a slow-spinning seventh have a tendency of needing to follow a cult, the stricter the better.

Balanced – Spins Harmoniously

Balance in the seventh chakra results in a magnetic personality, an understanding that one can achieve "miracles" in life, transcendence, and the feeling of peace from within. A balanced seventh chakra will yield a person who takes their time before making a decision, knowing that rash decisions are not beneficial. In looking at the mirror image of the lessons from the fast spinning chakra, hallucinations can be seen as a propensity toward visions that connect you to Universal love and abundance. The characteristic of religious fervor, in a slow spinning chakra, can lead you to an inclination towards theological or spiritual learning and even spiritual or religious leadership of some kind.

Letting the Old Self Die

The Sanskrit name for the seventh chakra is "Sahasrara", meaning "thousand-fold." The seventh chakra is represented by a 1,000-petaled lotus, which symbolizes the infinite nature of this chakra, and the connection with the Divine. Beginning in the pineal gland; which is close to the middle of the head and resembles a single, narrow cone opening upwards from the middle and crown of the head; this chakra is about death and rebirth. The lessons of this energy field show us that at times we have to let the old us die to be reborn once again. In many religions there is recognition of the importance of bringing awareness to this rite of passage. In Islam death is confronted five times a day, each time the devotee prays. In Buddhism death awareness is widely discussed. It is only in our western culture that we shy away from reflection of our own death. The seventh chakra beckons us to consider the death of our old self in order to make way for the Divine to come in and infuse each and every chakra with Her presence. We must make room by letting go of the old. In addressing the practice of death awareness, the Buddha has left us five contemplations, which he advised to reflect on frequently.

1. I am subject to aging. Aging is unavoidable.
2. I am subject to illness. Illness is unavoidable.

3.   I am subject to death. Death is unavoidable.
4.   I will grow different, separate from all that is dear and appealing to me.
5.   I am the owner of my actions, heir to my actions, born of my actions, related through my actions, and live dependent on my actions. Whatever I do, for good or for ill, to that will I fall heir.

These reflections have not been a major part of Buddhist practice in the western world. When Buddhism first got popular in the United States in the 1960's, people were coming out of the drug culture. Some looked at spirituality, and in particular at Buddhism, as another way to get high. They weren't looking for anything as intense as death mindfulness. They just wanted to escape.

But in countries where Buddhism has been established for centuries, the practice of death mindfulness is an ancient and honored tradition. In fact, there are some who regard it as the ultimate practice. The Buddha left behind this important statement: *"Of all the footprints, that of the elephant is supreme. Similarly, of all mindfulness meditation, that on death is supreme."* This is exactly why we need to confront the Dweller at the Threshold.

The Dweller at the Threshold

The Dweller can be defined as all of the forces of the lower nature. It is the sum total of the negative influences that are the result of the harmful thoughts and acts of one's accumulative age. It is an entity that dwells in one's mind that stands before the gate where Divinity enters our body and soul. It dwells in the shadow of the gateway of initiation. This Dweller is the sum total of all the personality characteristics which have remained unconquered and un-subdued, and which must be overcome before initiation can be taken. One way to silence the Dweller is to die. Just like birth, death (and I am not only talking about physical death, but rather the death of the ego) is a rite of passage.

Rites of Passage

Your first rite of passage was your own birth when you left your mother's womb and slid down the dark tunnel towards the unknown with only a promise of reunion. It was your first leap of faith. The pressure to leave increased with every hour and every minute. Your mother's body was expelling you, guiding you towards the dark tunnel. You were either ready and eager, or reluctant and stubborn. You either came with ease and grace, or with force and the help of knives or forceps. But you came, and eventually, sooner or later, you were held in your mother's arms and you were full of wonder, love, and unrelenting curiosity. The fetal part of you perished somehow and the new you began a slow journey toward independence.

From your mother's bosom you looked around and explored the new territory with all its people, places, and things; all the wonders you only imagined while in your mother's womb. Then came the day where you wanted to go and explore on your own. You tentatively left your mother's side and crawled into the unknown, running back as soon as something startled you. Slowly you gained more confidence and raised yourself from the ground and stepped forward. Another journey began, one that took you away from the mother and into your own life experience.

From birth to three years old you lived in your first chakra. Survival was your only task, yet you began to explore. Your aim was to become one with everything around you as you experienced the world through your close-knit tribe. You depended on your mother for everything and you focused only on your nucleolus, your home, family and your parent's friends.

From three to six you switched your focus to the second chakra. You needed to carve a place for yourself outside the family, outside your personal tribe. You slowly began to understand that things could be different -- even opposite from what you know. During this time you learned about relationships with others. This is the time when some of you began a formal process of socialization, such as going to school. Emotions were no longer related to your family and your immediate desires. You experienced emotions for the others, the strangers all around you. It's when you experienced the power of choice: be friends with this little girl and not that one; be accepted by this group and not the other one. You also became conscious of the "us" (children) and "them" (adults).

Between six and twelve you entered the realm of the third chakra. Here you began developing a sense of self. How you felt about yourself determined the quality of your life. Children between the ages of six and twelve years old don't grow as quickly as they do in their first six years. Similarly, their bodies aren't changing as dramatically as they will during adolescence. Therefore, growth during this stage is more internal. You are becoming a self. The ego has its first struggle to surmount, to win over your higher self. Even as your thinking became more complex, during this stage you still thought in concrete terms. You were most concerned with things that were "real" rather than with ideas. In the later part of middle childhood, you began to show the first signs of puberty. Your body began to develop the same proportions as an adult body. Your breasts may have grown buds and your hips widened, which lead you right into the fourth chakra, located in your heart - the love chakra, which takes center stage during the years between twelve and sixteen.

In this phase of your life you discovered the power of love, and of course you also experience its opposite. At this delicate time you dwelled in the central powerhouse of human energy. The middle chakra mediates between body and spirit. It is a very confusing time in a person's life. Life altering decisions are made in this time. As your body undergoes enormous changes, you thrived on arguments and discussions, and you likely needed to withdraw from your parents whom you felt inevitably did not understand you. Your child-self was about to perish and you were reaching the point where you would have to jump into adulthood. The need to rebel from the old familial ties was your catalyst to gain the courage to do so. Here your womb called on you with the sacred blood of your moon cycles. Here the Mother was showing you the birth-death-re-birth cycle of life.

As a young woman you prepared to flee the nest and be on your own. Some of you did it early, in your fifth chakra (the throat chakra). This chakra rules ages sixteen through nineteen. During the rebellion years the separation is dramatic, often exhibited in running away and feeling angry, sad, and forceful. This is the age of expression: of demanding the truth, speaking your mind, establishing your voice in the world. The separation might also have been subtler, such as going away to college and not coming back. Some ran away through drugs and/or alcohol. Maybe you did or considered taking these actions, or perhaps you were one of those who left between ages of nineteen and twenty-two as you were dwelling in the sixth chakra (third eye). In this phase of your life you might have had a vision, a glimpse of your future life. You chose to pursue what the vision promised and left the nest to follow a career or a calling. However, there are some of you who waited a bit longer and left in full seventh chakra (the crown chakra), between the ages of twenty three to twenty six, where your spiritual connection became strong, intensifying the connection with your higher self or the Divine.

For some, leaving the nest may have been done gracefully; you married, went to college, or found a roommate to share a home with and packed your bags with tears in your eyes, embracing your goodbyes. Others, like me, severed the cord painfully, crossed the great ocean and disappeared from their mother's sight for years. No matter when or how it happened, when the moment came you needed to let a previous phase of life simply "die" in its present incarnation. You took a big leap of faith into the unknown and experienced a rebirth as a separate individual. At this point the rites of passage cycle slows down till either you give birth to another human being or you enter the phase called menopause.

If you have given birth, then you know it is a rite that brings a woman full circle. In giving birth you re-experience your own birth, but this time from both perspectives. As you go through the actual labor and delivery your body and your unconscious self will recall your own birthing experience, and you may also come to understand your mother's perspective. If you did not get a chance to do this leap of faith consciously during pregnancy and birth, it will be re-proposed when you enter menopause. In this phase of a woman's life you will be asked to pause and take stock of all that has been, of your present life, and what lies ahead. Ultimately, all living creatures must face the rite of passage that is the death of the physical body. Many of us are totally unprepared for our loved one's passing let alone our own.

Rites of passage can be scary and intense, and can feel similar to jumping off from one ledge of the Grand Canyon to another. You can choose to use this intensity to make you stronger and prepare for all life's challenges. In order to jump from one ledge to the other you have to gather great courage.

Center yourself, take aim and run as fast as the wind will take you and jump, trusting in yourself, and the universe.

Focusing on the abyss between the two ledges (on what can go wrong) can only lead to fear, which in turn leads to procrastination and the release of a whole slew of chemicals in your body that can impede or slow your jump. One trick is not to look down, but forward. Preparation before the jump is essential.

The more difficult the jump the more you need to step back and ensure you have enough of a runway to gain the required speed. Metaphorically, this means going back through your life, looking to find what didn't work, letting go of what weighs you down, harnessing the good, and letting go of what no longer serves you. It means forgiving, releasing, rebirthing a new self, mending, and healing. This is all the work we have done thus far. You are also required to fall madly in love with yourself, for that kind of love is the one that will give you wings. It is only then that you are ready for the next jump, and what I call "the ultimate meditation."

The Ultimate Meditation

The seventh chakra aligns with the Tibetan Buddhist concept of Saṃsāra, which translates as *"he flows into himself,"* passing through states of existence, as a continuous flow repeating the cycle of birth, life, death and rebirth. In my years of studying the chakras, I've always read the seventh as the entrance of the godhead into the incarnate realm.

Through recognizing that the doorway between us and the universe, and all Divine energies, passes though this chakra, I've come to the conclusion that in order for God to come in I must make room. In Christian practices we are encouraged to say to God, *"thy will be done – not mine"*, in essence removing ourselves and offering our existence as a channel through which God can express it/her/him/self. *"Unless a grain of wheat falls into the earth and dies, it remains just a single grain; but if it dies, it bears much fruit"* (John 12:24.)

To allow a complete surrender of ego, I need to make room and therefore some of me must go – metaphorically die. But what parts are we talking about? Death in our western culture has a terribly negative connotation. We do everything possible to avoid it, even keeping the near-dead alive through machines rather than giving them the dignity of leaving this world consciously and with decorum. This is obviously a big and controversial subject. However, what I am talking about is not physical death, but the death of that which you have been so that you can infuse your rebirth with a renewed energy. Certainly, the old you must die – but that is not enough. In order to make room for the Divine we need to let go of all that attaches us to the past, present and future. Does simply letting go of what no longer serves me make enough room for God to be welcomed in? How do I go about proclaiming my death as I wait for my rebirth? And, how am I going to achieve this letting go? And, how can I incorporate this into my daily practice?

There are certainly more questions than answers in this regard, which is as it should be. Every one of us gets to find our own way through our personal death and rebirth cycle. And while each process is unique to the individual, I will share my own experience.

I decided that if I wanted to experience death I had to let go of that which increased my fear and diminished my self-esteem: those memories and patterns of the past that had played far too strong of a role in the making of who I was, and who I wanted to change, as well as those things I was so desperately attached to. The good, the bad, and the ugly. There came a need to go through the nine chakras of creation every day in my practice so that I could ensure all the work I had done would become part of me at a cellular level. I used the nine basic human rights in my meditation to give them time and attention, and to free any debris left over through the years. Yet, when it came to the seventh chakra, I resolved in finding a way to die each and every day, so I could be reborn, new and renewed.

To do this wholeheartedly I came up with a letting-go meditation I would perform daily. This meditation takes approximately five to ten minutes and is simple and quick, yet profoundly transformational. I use each inhale to harness all that I have and each exhale to let go of it all. When you read in the meditation below "I feel my right to be loved," I really want you to conjure up all people, places and things you love, and be willing with the exhale to let them all go. Yes, completely go. How would you live without your children? Your partner? To allow the Divine in completely you must let go completely. Only then will there be enough room.

Here is my daily meditation. I recommend you go slowly, as this mediation can be very emotional, and at times you may find you are not ready to let go of all that you hold dear. When I speak about letting go, just imagine that for one split second between inhalation and exhalation you are prepared to let go. For example, your sight, your hearing, and all of your sensory experience, all your loved ones, all that is... because that is what death is all about.

- Inhale – exhale – Coming into this moment
- Inhale – exhale – Opening up my seven chakras
- Inhale – Feeling my right to be here
- Exhale – Letting go all that is here
- Inhale – Feeling my right to my feelings
- Exhale – Letting go all of my feelings
- Inhale – Feeling my right to take the right actions

- ✦ Exhale – Letting go all of my actions
- ✦ Inhale – Feeling my right to love and be loved
- ✦ Exhale – Letting go everything and everyone I love
- ✦ Inhale – Feeling my right to speak and hear the truth
- ✦ Exhale – Letting go all of my words
- ✦ Inhale – Feeling my right to see and know the truth
- ✦ Exhale – Letting go of all that I see
- ✦ Inhale – Feeling my right to live a conscious life
- ✦ Exhale – Letting go of my life
- ✦ Inhale – Exhale – Feeling the void
- ✦ Inhale – Preparing for the healing
- ✦ Exhale – Allowing the light to come through me
- ✦ Inhale – Exhale – Preparing for my birth
- ✦ Inhale – Exhale – Coming into this moment
- ✦ Inhale – Exhale – Celebrating the moment

Now, it is time to place your crown chakra seed on your altar and nurture it with this prayer.

Closing Prayer
To thee, O Mother of my soul, I consecrate my life. Come to my side to receive the last breath of my past existence, and now help me bring this creation safely through this birthing each and every day into a new life.

The Right to My Divine Powers

Womb Conversation

"…if you remain in Me and My words remain in you, you may ask for anything you want, and it will be granted! You can pray for anything, and if you have faith, you will receive it" John 15: 7 - NLT

How can I help you open up to trusting in your own Divine powers?

Eighth Chakra - Divine Powers

Eight Chakra - The Right to Your Divine Power

The focus of this chakra is to find *your connection* with the sacredness of your everyday life, and to be open to the Divine messages you receive. I emphasize the words *your connection* for it is my belief that you should shape your own relationship with the Sacred regardless of what you have been told, what you have experienced in the past, and what your relationship is with organized religion. Some of us have been agnostics or atheists; some have had negative experiences with the word *God*. Some of us have been indoctrinated with an idea of God as a fierce father figure that would punish us if we did not follow His laws. Whatever your personal history is with the Divine it is my intention to inspire you to find the sacred connection with a power greater than yourself. Call it Mother Nature, the Universe, unconditional love, or whatever feels appropriate. The eight chakra hovers over your left shoulder. When we explore it we get to define and understand our Divine powers, and we get a glimpse at the world of the occult, of the supernatural, as we create a practice that exploits and exalts both light and darkness. We come to understand that there is no light without darkness, and no good without its opposite.

Spins Fast: In Excess, Congestion, Disharmony

Since this chakra is also the chakra that holds your karmic residue – those energy patterns that you have held onto for more than one lifetime – when it spins too fast you have the feeling that many people live in your head. Also, you can have megalomaniac as well as egomaniacal tendencies. Schizophrenia is one of the maladies of this chakra, as well as paranoia. The constant chatter of your mind takes your serenity away. It seems there is an entire committee living in your head and they are constantly judging and fear-mongering your thoughts.

Spins Slow: Deficiency, Depletion, Disharmony

When this center spins slowly you find yourself having serious doubts about the Divine and the concept of Mother Nature's love, specifically her love toward you. A slow-spinning eighth chakra can also bring nightmares, night terrors, and sleeplessness. You feel alone and abandoned. Skepticism reigns supreme and life seems futile. Staunch atheists and cult followers belong in this category. Either God does not exist or someone else has an exclusive relationship with the Divine and must be followed.

Balanced – Spins Harmoniously

When the eighth chakra begins to open up and expand, a new spiritual awareness takes shape. The individual senses himself or herself as part of a larger community of beings. You receive and embrace psychic messages whether they come as whispers, or in your dreams. Psychic abilities and the occult live in this chakra. To turn the fast-spinning and slow-spinning energies around you get to embrace the many people living in your head and love them as a group of teachers, and embrace your nightmares as precursors to prophetic dreams.

What is my Higher Power?

Eastern religions speak of the Divine not as an entity outside of us, but as something we are a part of, *"something that is closer than our hands and feet, nearer than our breath"* (The Quran). This abstract concept became very real when I felt my baby growing in my belly and I felt his touch and movements. When I speak of a Higher Power, I am referring to a Higher Love that encompasses all. Sometimes I call it God or Higher Power or Mother Nature. I encourage you to find your personal connection with a power greater than yourself. Being spiritually enlightened and leading a conscious life can be done as a Christian, Jew, Muslim, Hindu, Buddhist, and even an agnostic. What you call it, how you refer to it, or how you pray to it does not matter. What matters is that you feel the power of Creation within you and become one with this power. Seek your own relationship with the Divine. You don't need an intermediary. Let's take a look at your history and present belief about a power greater than yourself.

Here are the positive and negative characteristic of the God of my family's religion	How did those beliefs shape my relationship with the Divine?	What attributes does the God I want in my life have? How does this Divine Power support me?
Do I believe that the Divine cares about me? How do I know?	What helps me believe things will be OK?	What brings me hope?

How do I communicate with the goddess within?	How do I know when she is talking to me and how do I discern her voice from the other judgmental voices in my mind?	What are some of the messages I have received from my Higher Power?
Why is it essential to believe in a Higher Power?	What would my life be if I did not believe?	How do I feel when I believe there is a who, who loves me?

The Dicotomy of Divine Powers

I have been fascinated with the position of the eighth and ninth chakra, each hovering over one shoulder, and the common symbolic image depicting a devil and angel on our shoulders – the angel of conscience and the devil of temptation. These two archetypes, which have accompanied us throughout childhood in cartoons and fairytales, are often used for depicting the inner conflict of character. Usually, the angel is portrayed on (or hovering near) the right shoulder, and the devil or demon is on the left. The origins of such lore date back to the non-canonical Early Christian book, *The Shepherd of Hermas*, from around A.D. 140-150, in which it is written, *"There are two angels with a man—one of righteousness, and the other of iniquity."*

In Islamic belief, similarly, there are two figures called Kiraman Katibin, two angels residing on either shoulder, which record our good and bad deeds. In Islam, there is no mention of interaction between humans and these entities, i.e. we are not told to listen to them. Instead, Hermas suggests we understand both angels, but only trust the Angel of Righteousness. This idea of seeing through the filter of right and wrong, darkness and light, is responsible for much personal and global dis-ease. When we look at the gifts of the night, the beauty of darkness, the shades of grey and the power of magic, we can see that this energy hovering on our left shoulder is a strong and powerful entity.

In essence, good and evil are coming from the same basic source, God's Will. Very little in nature is either good or bad. Something becomes good or bad based upon how it is used. Massive harm and terrific evil have been done to countless people over the millennia in the name of what was thought to be the ultimate good. Nothing is simply all good or all bad. To illustrate this concept let's look at something we usually take for granted:

- **Altruism** is seen as a saintly trait. Without it we can be unaware of other's needs. However, with too much of it we can ignore our own needs and end up dishonoring ourselves.
- **Selfishness** if often considered a negative trait. Too much of it can result in lack of sensibility towards others, too little and you become extremely insecure, abiding by other people preferences.

Similarly, Divine powers can be perceived as dangerous. The word power is often interpreted as having negative connotations. Political, personal, and physical powers misused for the wrong reasons can become instruments of subjugation and malice that can ultimately hurt. However, harnessing our Divine powers can become an instrument of love and healing. Historically, Divine powers have only been claimed by the occultist. Magi, witches and alchemists dared to channel supernatural powers.

The Occult

In proclaiming, *"I have the right to my Divine Powers,"* we come to a dilemma: Are we embarking on a dangerous journey? If we choose to use this power with conscientiousness we can perform good deeds for others, yet we might forget ourselves and our needs along the way. On the other hand, if we use these powers selfishly are we bound to do harm by manipulating people and situations for our own good? Furthermore, when we speak about Divine powers are we experimenting in magic and the occult? Does acknowledging them or dabbling with them take us into forbidden territory? Is the belief that you have Divine Powers a dark and dangerous path?

Too often the occult and the devil have been used as synonymous of one another. Practicing psychic abilities, harnessing metaphysical powers, and/or not speaking with God through an appropriate intermediary (priest, guru, monk, or rabbi) are also seen as borderline evil. We are taught that the occult works with the dark side and is dangerous. However, the more we look at the tenements of the occult the more we discover the forward thinking of those who practiced it.

The occult includes many practices and belief systems. These beliefs are usually based in the idea that everything is or contains energy (an unquantifiable energy), and one can access, change, channel and/or manipulate this energy (or force) for the purposes of gaining information, healing, or bringing a desired situation or thing into material reality. These tenements are similar to the principles of quantum physics and epigenetics. By denying the duality perceived in the concept of good and evil, darkness and light, we reach a place of infinite possibilities. A place where we become vehicles for the greater good and are instruments of God's will for us.

Divine Powers

What does it means to have Divine Powers? Our body is already a channel of Divine Powers. Have you noticed how a wound can heal itself without any help from you? Do you realize that without your prompt your heart beats; your lungs, liver, stomach, and kidneys function as they were designed? Our physical bodies are comprised of approximately 100 trillion living cells; we replace 300 million cells every minute. Now that is a great example of your Divine Powers at work since your inception! Your body is a wondrous creation and so are your mind and spirit. Within you there is a physician, a pharmacist, a therapist, a priestess, a shaman, and a healer on call 24/7. All you have to do is acknowledge their presence, harness their wisdom, and become part of their mission.

Having consciousness of the powers already at work in our bodies, we now turn to our mind and spirit and their ability to channel Divine Powers. When we encourage and develop the opening of the eighth chakra we nurture our psychic abilities. Numerous scientific investigations have been made into the validity of these abilities. You have probably already experienced psychic abilities in your life. It just takes a little practice to fully cultivate confidence in psychic information and trust that it isn't just your imagination. When you are looking for answers, the first thing that usually comes to mind is your gut reaction (second chakra), then logic takes over. Each of us has psychic abilities that are stronger in some areas and weaker in others. These special powers that you possess can make great things happen with the right combination of commitment, patience, effort, and the proper guidance from a spiritual midwife.

Look at this list and ask yourself when and if you have experienced any of the following:

1. *Intuition.* Every person is born with a natural intuitive ability. Women have been recognized as having heightened intuition by nature. Have you ever known who was calling on the phone before you even answered it? Have you known what someone would say before they actually said it?

2. *Déjà Vu.* Have you ever felt like you've already experienced something before you actually did? This is called Déjà Vu, when you have the strong sensation that an event currently being experienced has been

experienced in the past, whether it has actually happened or not.

3. *Telepathy.* Have you been so connected to a girlfriend you just needed a look and you knew what she was thinking? Have you been in love with someone and so connected you finished each other sentences?

4. *Visions.* Do you get visions from time to time? Have you ever had a dream that eventually came true, or that was a premonition of things to come? Receiving visions, through dreams or otherwise, is also a strong sign of your Divine Powers.

5. *Have you found yourself simply knowing without explanation?* Are there moments that you just simply have a gut feeling about something without having logical explanation for it? This type of scenario is a clear-cut indication of your Divine Powers.

6. *Self-healing.* Have you ever trusted that an ailment could be coaxed away by a positive disposition on your part and it happened? Would you not call that Divine intervention?

7. *Self-awareness.* Have you ever felt part of a bigger design? Experienced oneness with all living things?

8. *Manifesting.* Have you ever set a seemingly impossible goal and obtained it?

9. *Womb potentiality.* Whether you have had a child or not, when you acknowledge that you possess the ultimate instrument of creation you feel closer to God who creates all living life.

Once we have awareness of our innate Divine Powers, we can turn to nurturing them.

Nurturing our Divine Powers

Divine Power is sustained through being one with Mother Earth. A woman becomes enlivened when she honors and surrenders to the innate rhythms of her body and her psyche. In order to develop and nurture your Divine Powers you must be committed to yourself 100%, which means you get to:

+ *Let go of your conditioning.* Release past lovers, past relationships, and past history. Negative thoughts hamper psychic abilities. Trust in the messages that are whispered to you. Believe that you can be a conduit for the Divine to bring good news into this world.

+ *Align* with the ebbing and flowing, with the waxing and waning of the moon's sacred cycles within your womb.

+ *Be who you truly are.* Be the love that you are. Melt with your softness, your strength, and your power. Silence the naysayers.

+ *Slow down.* Feel the earth's wild and powerful heartbeat within your womb.

+ *Listen.* Hear what your womb has to say. Speak to her often. Invite her into your heart. Embody her wisdom, her love, her vivacity and warmth.

+ *Expand your imagination by using self-hypnosis.* See yourself exactly where you want to be, imagine every detail. Smell, taste, see, and hear your goals. Do this often and with the feeling that "it has already come to pass."

+ *Awaken your sensual nature.* Dance with the flow of life. Open your heart to the divine flow that pulses through your yoni, your womb, your belly, your breasts, and your heart.

✦ **Believe in the goodness of the Divine.** In the 60s, a new word was coined – pronoia – it is the opposite of paranoia. It means that the universe is conspiring for your own good. Believe it and only positive energies will speak to you.

Meditate. Prayer is talking. The conversations we have with God should be filled with expressions of gratitude to the universe for all the good we have already received. Meditation is listening. This is where you stop making noise and give God a chance to talk back.

Practice

At times the path to awakening our Divine Powers can seem lonely – especially when the people around you are not on the same path. In ignorance or fear, people might look at you as mad or pretentious. Some might even make fun of you. Indeed, there is some madness in awakening these powers in a world in which such practices are reserved for the "occultist."

The renowned Hindu mystic, Muktanada, once said that it is far better never to set foot upon the spiritual path. However, once you do, it is far better that you never get off. He said that this path can be seen as a path to madness, for is not the one we call mad the one who is different from the norm? Carolyn Myss tells us:

> What then is spiritual madness? It is the experience of encountering that which another has not yet realized, yet you know is "real." The "real" that you encounter is of such profound

*power that it crushes the world of illusion—or
a part of it – in which you reside. Madness
is the result of encountering the realm of the
"original" – a truth or realization that has yet
to incarnate.*

If you have read books about becoming one with the universe, such as the *Celestine Prophecy* or the *Power of Now*, you've learned of the moment in which plants, animals, and even rocks can speak to you in harmony. You may even have experienced this yourself, and heard the painful cries of Mother Nature. It is the madness that tells you to wake up one day and do the impossible, to follow a seemingly unobtainable goal, to heed the call that was whispered to you in a dream or during a meditation. Madness can come from ignoring the message on the one hand, or responding to the call on the other, in a world where doing so makes you an outcast and unrecognizable to yourself. That is why the path of entering your soul is so dangerous – for once you know you cannot undo the knowing. Once you hear the messages in your heart you cannot silence them.

The work that we've come to do is not our own, but the work of the Universe. Thus, channeling our Divine Power is neither good nor evil, but simply the nature of our being. We clear the eighth chakra to become the vessel through which Divine Powers are channeled. We all have these powers, but our abilities usually lie hidden until they are activated. As with any skill, Divine Powers develop with regular use and diminish with lack of use. They can be learned by anyone who takes the time and effort to learn them, and that time and effort is always better when coupled with a commitment to living consciously. Immediately following my divorce, I had to find a way to support my children. I was between careers, so I worked as a psychic for three years of my life. I used to go to an office and for eight hours a day and read tarot cards, the I Ching, or give an astrology reading. My psychic abilities increased exponentially in this period of my life by simply being used and exercised daily within a certain discipline. By the end of the three years all I had to do is hear someone's voice and I would immediately get a message about their life's challenges and a glimpse of the solutions that were available. Yes solutions, for there are always choices in life.

How do we encourage and practice opening up our soul to hear God's messages to us, and how do we turn those messages into our Divine Powers? All you need to do is start believing and trusting in these tiny whispers on the edge of your conscious thought. Once you do, they will become stronger and clearer to discern from your everyday thoughts. Just as you'd get better at playing piano the more you practice, you can get better at this if you incorporate this listening into your daily practice.

Divine Power is taking care of us because we do not exist as separate entities from the universe. We are not apart from it, but a part of it. The universe is taking care of itself all the time, and therefore when we place ourselves in its care, we will never experience any lack. So, when we ask or we manifest something that seems like magic, we do so because we access the Divine, which is already within us. In fact, it *is* us. We are not living our own lives; the universe is living through us.

Recently, I learned a new word – grit. I have immediately fallen in love with it. It means passion for a particular long-term goal or end state coupled with a powerful motivation to achieve the respective objective. Grit is conceptualized as a stable trait that does not require immediate positive feedback. Having grit means focusing on a goal wholeheartedly. No set back is seen as a deterrent, but a powerful step back readying you for a comeback. If you approach interest in your Divine powers with grit you cannot fail.

Now, it is time to place your dream chakra seed on your altar and nurture it with this prayer.

> ### Closing prayer
> *Thank you for the capacity to feel gratitude at all times. Thank you for the opportunity to feel gratitude at all times. Dear God, thank you for your pure presence radiant in my own heart. Truly, thank you for the infinity of your presence.*

The Right to be One with the Miraculous

Womb Conversation

As I trust and align with pure energy, I become aware of the law of Divine oneness. The universe is self-correcting and self-organizing as I tap into oneness through love.

Can you see the infinite possibilities?
Can you give me my first clue?

Ninth Chakra – Incarnation

Ninth Chakra - The Right to Be One with the Miraculous

The ninth chakra is the one in which all Christ/Buddha/ Mohammed consciousness lay veiled, waiting to be unconfined and used in the outer and inner worlds. The ninth chakra, unlike the others, does not have characteristics of spinning slow, or fast. This chakra has neither duality; nor the trinity of slow, fast, and balanced. It is quite challenging to even speak about it since it contains an ineffable quality. Seeing it as the angel on the right shoulder can help us begin to grasp the concept of being closer to God. That angel is a part of the inverted funnel that allows us to imagine spirit flowing through us and becoming incarnate within us through our seventh chakra. It can help us to know deeply and believe completely, at every level of our being, that we are not separate from God, that we are one with the Divine. Such knowledge can heal us and the world entirely.

Most spiritual leaders speak of the importance of living with the awareness of our oneness with God. In theory, if every human being would live and act and feel with this awareness, the planet would heal, species that are now facing extinctions would survive, there would be no poverty or starvation, wars would end and love would reign. If we incorporate the belief that we are all made up of the same fabric, that all things are as important as one another, we would no longer need to fight for our survival. The ninth chakra is the final chakra that reflects this truth. This is the gateway to the consciousness of oneness. It takes years and even life times to reach this potentiality. We can sometimes get a glimpse of it, and when we do we are transformed even if just for one moment.

If you've experienced this unity you most certainly were in a trance and may even have seen some kind of intricate soul-circuitry, or matrix. This is what some call an "aha experience," that moment in life where you feel connected to the Divine source.

The Right to be One with God/ Spirit/The Miraculous

When we believe we are separate from Spirit we remain ill at ease, frightened, weak, powerless, tied to the past, resentful, stuck, and hopeless. This separation from Spirit leaves us unable to release the powerful healing life force in us.

Many of us were born into religions that claimed God is somewhere up there on a mountaintop, or in the heavens, looking down on us, and in order to access that God we need to go outside ourselves. The spiritual path directs us in the opposite direction – it encourages us to look for God within. Yet, they both teach to *Know Thyself*. The deeper you go within yourself, the more you will know yourself, and in turn come to know the God within you. It takes God out of the realm of abstract concepts, and makes God a living entity inside us, moving through us, being us. This awareness begs a few questions, "What reverence do you have for God's creation?

How would you talk to yourself and others if you addressed the God within? What vision do you have of God's life through you?

What would happen if everyone would look upon God's creations as his or her daughter, son, mother, father, lover or friend? What if we were to look upon everyone with compassion, even when we disagree with him or her, even when we deeply condemn some of their behaviors? If we could get to this level of compassion for all beings we could heal so many things in the world.

All spiritual paths regardless of how they portray God teach us the importance to treat others, as we'd like to be treated. This ancient wisdom, known as the golden rule, refers to the ninth chakra's concept of oneness.

The Golden Rule

The Golden Rule is the bedrock of religious understanding. It is expressed almost word for word in every religion. Here are quotes from many paths to God:

> *Do unto others as you would have them do unto you, for this is the law and the prophets.* Christianity - Matthew 7:12, Luke 6:31

> *What is hurtful to yourself do not to your fellow man. That is the whole of The Torah and the remainder is but commentary.* Judaism - Shabbath (also Rabbi Hillel)

> *Do unto all men as you would they should unto you, and reject for others what you would reject for yourself.* Islam - Mishkat-el-Masabih

Hurt not others with that which pains yourself.
Buddhism

Tzu Kung asked: "Is there any one principle upon which one's whole life may proceed?" Confucius replied: "Is not Reciprocity such a principle?- what you do not yourself desire, do not put before others." Confucianism - Analects 15.23

This is the sum of all true righteousness - Treat others, as thou wouldst thyself be treated. Do nothing to thy neighbor, which hereafter Thou wouldst not have thy neighbor do to thee. Hinduism - Mahabharata (Ganguli, Book 13 CXIII)

Treat others as thou wouldst be treated thyself. Sikhism - Guru Angad (Macauliffe vol 2, p.29)

A man should wander about treating all creatures as he himself would be treated. Jainism - Sutrakritanga Sutra 1.11.33

Regard your neighbor's gain as your own gain, and regard your neighbor's loss as your own loss, even as though you were in their place. Taoism - Tai-Shang Kan-Ying Pien

Ascribe not to any soul that which thou wouldst not have ascribed to thee. Bahá'í - Bahá'ulláh

To live from the ninth chakra is a goal, which very few can obtain. It is the utopic world of Plato, the paradise described in the scriptures, nirvana, and the impossible dream. Yet, it is a goal that some of us aim for. The Golden Rule is the practical means to reach this goal and not a vague ideal. It embodies the deepest aspirations of humanity. It serves as the basis for all that is positive and lasting in human life. This is no longer a hippy-dippy concept, today science shares the same principles.

Science and Spirit

> "Science without religion is lame, religion without science is blind."
>
> - Albert Einstein

The separation between science and spirituality is crumbling. We can no longer simply embrace Darwinian theory that states that everything is matter, and that we came together accidentally through a series of evolutionary mistakes and coincidences. Nor can we simply say that God created all and there is no need to understand the how or why. After Darwin, Newton stated that everything was made of what, at the time, was believed to be a solid matter (the atom). Later, Einstein would prove that atoms could be broken down and analyzed further, that the subatomic particles which formed the atom were pure energy. Today, it is theorized by quantum physicists that although these atoms may seem from a physical point of view to be changeable types of energy (due to their varying structures and the numbers of sub-atomic particles which comprise them), when analyzed and broken down into their purest form they can influence and even create reality. Furthermore, quantum theorists state that, at the core, all matter is made up of "One Energy."

Many philosophers and spiritual teachers are coming together and agreeing on a few basic assumptions:

+ *"Matter cannot process meaning,* [by itself]*"* mathematical physicist Roger Penrose and Professor of Philosophy at the University of California, Berkeley.

+ *"There is an undivided wholeness and an implicate order, from which arises the explicate order of the universe as we experience it."* David Joseph Bohm theoretical physicist. In other words, everything is made from an undivided wholeness (one energy – anima mundi – uterus mundi) and from an intrinsic design.

+ "Consciousness is the quality *or state of awareness or, of being aware of an external object or something within oneself."* Merriam-Webster.

+ *"The purpose of consciousness is to make the unconscious conscious"* Carl Jung.

+ *"Creativity is purposeful."* Quantum physicist P. K. Aravind.

For centuries many avatars and spiritual leaders have preached that spirit and matter are intertwined, that they need one another to exist. They've spoken of integration through energy, and almost unanimously told us about the need for transcendence and love. To live a conscious life, to become fully aware, they tell us we have two important tools at our disposal: meditation/prayer, and love. Love, an emotion and not a thought, becomes the thread weaving humanity and God together in wholeness. As a womb-carrying human you can use the Uterus Mundi as the metaphorical energy and your physical womb to co-create your life and purpose.

Cultivation and Practice

Thus far, I have taken you on a journey to discover your unconscious beliefs, feelings, actions, words, vision, knowledge, and divine potentiality through the nine chakras of creation, to help you shed light into your unconscious mind. I have held the space, as I do when I work as a doula, for you to create your purpose of bringing your unconscious self into the light. I've encouraged you at the end of each chakra to place an object onto your altar representing a seed of inspiration that came from the work done on that chakra. Now, we go about the fertilization of each seed.

In the Uterus Mundi, the place where all life is generated and where all seeds can be planted to create everything and anything we want to manifest, the eighth and ninth chakras are metaphorically represented as the two ovaries, one on the left and one on the right. These ovaries carry the eggs/consciousness of Ultimate Creation. Once one of these eggs is released it embarks on a journey through the chakras and lands in the Uterus Mundi to be fertilized by the seed/purpose/intention. The fertilization of these eggs comes from the conscious placement of these seeds.

The highest of all possible human goals is the attainment of mindfulness through a spiritual awakening. A spiritual awakening is an ultimate state of peace in which all obstacles obscuring the mind have been removed, and all good qualities such as wisdom and compassion have been fully developed. However, we cannot reach this ultimate goal merely by waiting for it. We need to commit to a life free from past influences and future expectations, caring deeply about the understanding of the self, and excited to be the creator of our present.

I am sure you have heard that you reap more than you sow. In fact, I believe you will reap an over abundance of negative things if you sow negative seeds. When you sow seeds of compassion, positive energy, respect for yourself and others, you will reap an over abundance of good things. Many of us get lost in the journey, impatient, longing for immediate results. The path is not for the soft-hearted, the work is hard, even wrenching at times. We live in a fast-food society, with expectations of instant gratification. Patience is a rare virtue that always rewards those who practice it. That is why I find myself often in need of a reminder in the form of a good book or a workshop. Even though I am a writer and leader of workshops, I need constant prompting to continue on my journey towards oneness with God.

In cultivating our spirit, we are also reminded that the quality of the harvest depends on the quality of the soil. In Mark, Chapter 4, we read the following:

> "Listen! A sower went out to sow. And as he sowed, some seed fell along the path, and the birds came and devoured it.
>
> Other seed fell on rocky ground, where it did not have much soil, and immediately it sprang up, since it had no depth of soil. And when the sun rose it was scorched, and since it had no root, it withered away.
>
> Other seed fell among thorns, and the thorns grew up and choked it, and it yielded no grain. And other seeds fell into good soil and produced grain, growing up and increasing and yielding thirtyfold and sixtyfold and a hundredfold."

The soil I refer to are the conditions, intentions and purposes of a person's heart, the care taken of their body temple, the commitment to their practice and a healed womb. To learn more deeply about sowing seeds and getting ready for harvest, all we need to do is observe a good farmer and the care she has for her crops. Here are some basic principles followed in cultivation:

1. *Choose good seeds.* Choose self-care, love, joy, peace, patience, kindness, goodness, artistry, gentleness, faithfulness, and charity.
2. *Prepare your fields with awareness.* Heal the past, clean out the weeds, turn the soil of past experiences, let go of all that crowds your heart, mind and soul.
3. *Give your crops plenty of room to grow.* Life brings many opportunities our way. Some are bad, some are good, some are better, and some are best. Occupy most of your time in the "better and best" activities.
4. *Water and fertilize.* Invest time in meditation, prayer, journaling, and in nature. Try to limit your media consumption and spend time in good stewardship.
5. *Never tramp mud into the house.* Gossip, complaints and victim behavior muddy up the path. Be conscious of your words.
6. *Get rid of the pests that destroy your plants.* Eliminate bad attitudes and bad influences. Limit or forgo mind-altering substances. Stay in the present, even if it means feeling your feelings.
7. *Support your plants as needed.* Use appreciation, gratitude, and communication. Ask and offer help.
8. *Uproot weeds frequently.* Practice soul cleaning every time you feel an old worn-out habit surface. Practice understanding instead of blame, owning your part

instead of taking someone else's inventory. Shut off self-deprecation and belittling voices.

9. ***Prepare for the harvest.*** Make sure you feel you have a right to reap your rewards. Make sure you have the room in your heart, mind, and soul for the success that is about to abound in your life. And, be grateful for the small and large fruits of your labor.

As the seed is genetically coded to become a splendid flower, and the embryo is coded to become a precious baby, you are spiritually coded to be a superb expression of the Mother God. The magnificence that you are is the gift you have come to give the world.

It is in the journey that we realize the beauty of duality, which is our experience of life. It is at the end of our journey, our death, that we go back (physically as well as mentally and spiritually) to the dissolution of who we are to become one with the whole.

The ninth chakra brings us back to the concept of unity we touched upon in the first chakra, where we discovered how we are connected to all our ancestry and ultimately to mother earth. In our ninth chakra we get a glimpse at our connection with the Divine. It brings this journey full circle where the Divine is no longer a concept that lives outside of ourselves, but is within the chalice of all creation called the Uterus Mundi. To feel oneness with God, the Source, and Mother Nature is no small task. It can take a lifetime (or more) to barely experience the complete oneness. Yet, we all have had a glimpse of this gift. If you ever want to call on the experience of oneness go into total gratitude for everything that surrounds you and you will get a glimpse of it. Your heart feels full of love and joy, and everything feels right with the world. To me, this is a state of Grace of oneness with God. My wounded self can never feel oneness with God, because it is a fabrication of my mind, not God's creation. Only through healing, embracing, and having compassion for myself can I glimpse at this nirvana. The powerful soul-based healing we receive in this journey to oneness, allows you to co-create at a physical, emotional, and spiritual level for yourself and those you love. When you realize that you are the creator of your own life you experience a life-changing understanding of your unique purpose, and how to live it with passion, aliveness, and freedom each and every day.

Now it is time to place your God chakra seed on your altar and nurture it with this prayer.

> ### Closing Prayer
> "Do not believe in anything simply because you have heard it. Do not believe in anything simply because it is spoken and rumored by many. Do not believe in anything simply because it is found written in your religious books. Do not believe in anything merely on the authority of your teachers and elders. Do not believe in traditions because they have been handed down for many generations. But after observation and analysis, when you find that anything agrees with reason and is conducive to the good and benefit of one and all, then accept it and live up to it." Hindu Prince Gautama Siddhartha, the founder of Buddhism, 563-483 B.C.

Seeds of Creations

The function of our conversations with the womb is to enable us to heal and detach from the past and the future, to heal in the now and savor the moment for what is, not what it could be or what it was. The womb is the ultimate source of a human being's inner security; it is the place she can lean on at any time and return to for endless replenishment and nourishment. The more connected you are with your womb, the clearer you will be able to hear the purity of its voice. The more this voice is listened to and acted upon, the more it will reveal. The nature of this voice can be soft and quiet, or it can be unexpectedly revolutionary and seemingly against conventional wisdom. Our womb has been known throughout the ages to be The Oracle. Like learning a new language it takes practice to tune-in and listen to this oracle, and the more we are able to do this, the more we can reclaim our self-governing inner authority.

In the same way that a developing fetus does not really look like a baby in the early months of gestation, you and I look nothing like what God ultimately intends for us. Even in the most trying of situations, we can rest knowing that, in comparison to eternity, the time we spend in the world's womb is momentary. I see my time on Earth for what it is – the necessary path on my way to heaven.

Healing the womb is as vital to men as it is to women, for in doing this the age-old wounds that reside in both male and female consciousness are returned to balance. The womb is the chamber of transformation of all energies and patterns, including those we like to harness and those we need to discard.

Opening your chakras starts with the first step of recognizing that you have an energy imbalance. If you find yourself in a crisis, or stuck in a rut, you can use the Nine Chakras of Creation as a query. I found that after this deep query (which at times took days, months, and even years) I started to incorporate the nine chakras of creation as a quick list I could run through to discover in which chakra a particular energy I was experiencing resonated and how I could bring light to an unconscious malaise I was experiencing. To do this you can run through each chakra asking the questions below as if in a conversation with your creative and nurturing womb. Remember to quiet your chattering mind and only wait for the feelings that surface. Think of the situation you want to get clarity about and ask the following questions. I have added an example to further explain the methodology.

Let's say I have had a rouse with a loved one, their words hurt me at a deep level and I feel our relationship is over. Here's how I'd start:

1. **Do I belong here?**
   a. When I am in this relationship do I feel I belong? Is there any influence by my family, or my community that is coloring the feelings that I have right now about this person?
2. **How do I feel?**
   a. Do I share my truth with this person, or am I holding on to this relationship in fear of

abandonment and/or in fear that my feelings are not important and will not be heard?

3. **What actions are my responsibility?**

   a. As the adage goes it takes two to tango. What actions did I take that are responsible for what has happened today or currently in this relationship?

4. **Do I feel loved, have I been loving?**

   a. Do I feel loved by this person? If not why not? If I believe I am a lovable person why am I so attached to what this person thinks of me? Why do I love this person? Why am I in a loving relationship with them?

5. **Was I impeccable with my words, did I share my truth?**

   a. Have I told them the truth, have I told myself the truth about this relationship? In the argument was I listening to what they were saying or did I jump to think about my rebuttal? Did I allow for silence? Did I immediately demand for a solution or did I allow time and space to change the moment?

6. **What is my ultimate vision for this situation?**

   a. Do I have a particular vision about this relationship and am I trying to fit this reality into an abstract vision? Am I appreciating what is? Can I see myself growing from this?

7. **Am I able to let go completely of any expectations? Can I see this situation as new?**

   a. Does my fear of being alone have anything to do with what just happened? Am I afraid to let go of my opinion and allow someone else to differ from me even though we stay together? What am I holding on so tight to?

8. **Have I forgotten my Divine Powers?**
   a. Does this situation make me feel powerless? Have I forgotten of my Divine Powers which can help me through anything in life? Have I listened and asked my Uterus Mundi, my womb, for the right answers?

9. **Do I feel one with this situation? Do I feel separate? Have I given as I like to receive?**
   a. Have I connected to gratitude? Have I thought of this person as a part of me? Have I treated this person as I'd want to be treated? Have I looked at this person as an expression of God?

This questionnaire is an example of how to use the nine chakras to run through a particular situation where you need clarity. You could literally run any situation through this system.

This will automatically bring you back to the concept discussed in the final ninth chakra where we realize that our only creative purpose for existence is to make the unconscious conscious and co-create our universe. I encourage you to keep conversing with your womb on a daily basis. She is your best friend, your confidant, your maiden, mother and crone.

A Final Note

At the beginning of this book, I told you that at the end you would be asked to do something in your journal that would help reveal your life's purpose. If you have followed the suggestions at the beginning of this book, you have both created an altar (or purse) to represent you womb and you have started a journal to record your discoveries and conversations with your womb. I'd like you now to go into the journal and circle or highlight the words you have repeated the most. Count the reoccurrences and list these words from most repeated to least.

Now, if the message these words are suggesting to you is not immediately apparent, ask your womb to tell you what it is about these words that you need to know. For instance, I had a woman who found that the most recurrent word in her diary was *listen*, and so in listening she quickly realized that her life's purpose was to become a therapist as she simply loved listening and helping other people by sharing the tools she had learned by listening to her own voice. Another found that the word *writing* was very prominent and discovered her long-lost love for the written word. She is now in the process of writing her first book.

In several of my workshops, when we did this exercise women found love as the most recurring word and would come to me and ask, "How would love be interpreted as a life purpose?" I would tell them that love is the ultimate purpose of life, and to focus on how they could practice loving they should look to the other recurring words for clues. In the end, the more questions we ask our womb the livelier our conversations will be. We have created several tools that will help you on the journey to heal, unblock, and harness the Nine Chakras of Creation. To learn more visit my website: ConversationsWithTheWomb.com.

Chronological Bibliography

Write It Down, Make It Happen: Knowing What You Want and Getting It Henriette Anne Klauser - Fireside Books; 1st edition (January 2001)

Painless Childbirth: An Empowering Journey Through Pregnancy and Birth by Giuditta Tornetta Cumberland House Publishing – (May 2008)

Women's Bodies Women's Wisdom - Dr. Christiane Northrup – Random House (May 2010)

The Wandering Womb: A Cultural History of Outrageous Beliefs About Woman - Lana Thompson (Prometheus Books (February 1999)

The Woman in the Body: A Cultural Analysis of Reproduction - Emily Martin - Beacon Press (August 2001)

The Bhagavad Gita - Simon Brodbeck (Author, Introduction), Juan Mascaro (Translator) Penguin Classic (January 2003)

Getting the Love You Want Dr. Harville Hendrix St. Martin's Griffin; Revised and Updated edition (April 1, 2010)

The Book of Wisdom: The Heart of Tibetan Buddhism. Commentaries on Atisha's Seven Points of Mind Training - Osho - Osho Media International; Revised Edition (February 2010)

On Grief and Grieving: Finding the Meaning of Grief Through the Five Stages of Loss - Elisabeth Kubler-Ross and David Kessler - Scribner; Reprint edition (July 2005)

Living With an Empty Chair - A Guide Through Grief - Dr. Roberta Temes - New Horizon Press Publishers (1989)

Primal Man: The New Consciousness - Dr. Arthur Janov - Little, Brown Book Group; 1 edition (January 1, 1991)

Man's Search for Meaning - Viktor E. Frankl - Beacon Press; 1 edition (June 2006)

The Spirit of Kaizen: Creating Lasting Excellence One Small Step at a Time - Robert Maurer - McGraw-Hill; 1 edition (October 2012)

The Biology of Belief - Bruce H. Lipton Ph.D. - Hay House (January 2013)

Loving What Is: Four Questions That Can Change Your Life - Byron Katie and Steven Mitchell - Harmony; 1 edition (May 2002)

A Course In Miracles - Foundation For Inner Peace - Foundation for Inner Peace; 3 Combined edition (May 2008)

Eleven Minutes - Paulo Coelho (Author), Margaret Jull Costa (Translator) - Harper Perennial; Reprint edition (March 2005)

I Thought It Was Just Me (but it isn't): Making the Journey from "What Will People Think?" to "I Am Enough" - Brené Brown - Gotham; Reprint edition (December 2007)

The Eagle's Gift - Carlos Castaneda - Washington Square Press; Reprint edition (December 1991)

The Essential Rumi - Jalal al-Din Rumi (Author), John Moyne (Translator) - HarperCollins e-books; Reprint edition (September 2010)

Callings: Finding and Following an Authentic Life - Gregg Michael Levoy - Harmony (September 1998)

The Art of Loving - Erich Fromm - Bantam Books; Highlighting edition (1963)

Ask and It Is Given: Learning to Manifest Your Desires - Esther Hicks and Jerry Hicks - Hay House (2004) (January 2010)

As a Man Thinketh - James Allen - Encore Books (September 2013)

Willpower - Roy F. Baumeister and John Tierney - Penguin Books; Reprint edition (September 2011)

This Is Your Brain on Music: The Science of a Human Obsession - Daniel J. Levitin - Plume/Penguin; 1 Reprint edition (August 2007)

No Future Without Forgiveness - Desmond Tutu - Image (October 2000)

Entering the Castle: An Inner Path to God and Your Soul - Caroline Myss - Atria Books; Reprint edition (January 2008)